A SENSE OF HISTORY

Expansion, Trade and Industry

JAMES MASON

ANGELA LEONARD
Assessment Consultant

 LONGMAN

Acknowlegments

We are grateful to the following for permission to reproduce copyright photographs:

Bodleian Library, Oxford, page 50; 'From the Collections of Bolton Museums and Art Gallery', page 33; Bradford Art Galleries and Museums, page 121; British Library, London/Bridgeman Art Library, London, page 82; British Museum/Bridgeman, page 71; Christie's, London/Bridgeman, page 53; Guildhall Library, Corporation of London/Bridgeman, pages 4, 7, 89; Luton Museum, Bedfordshire/Bridgeman, page 103; Royal Holloway College and Bedford New College, Surrey/Bridgeman, page 14; 'By permission of the British Library', page 44; Bristol Museums and Art Gallery, page 84; British Waterways Archives, page 32; Cadbury Limited, page 51; J. Allan Cash Photolibrary, pages 68, 70 (below); Chelmsford County Library, page 127 (above); 'Viscount Coke and the Trustees of the Holkham Estate', page 29 (below); Cyfarthfa Castle Museum and Art Gallery, Merthyr Tydfil, page 24; Dartford Borough Museum, page 66; Derby Museums and Art Gallery, page 45; Robert Fleming Holdings Limited, page 61; Hulton Deutsch Collection Limited, pages 9, 22 (above), 29 (above), 75, 91, 93, 106, 113, 119, 128 (below); Michael Holford, page 72; Illustrated London News Picture Library, page 8; Elton Collection: Ironbridge Gorge Museum Trust, pages 16, 33, 98, and Ironbridge Gorge Museum Trust, page 19; A. F. Kersting, page 70 (above); © Manchester City Art Galleries, page 108; Mander and Mitchenson Theatre Collection, page 65 (left); Mansell Collection, pages 5, 15, 46, 90, 95 (above and below), 99, 123; Mary Evans Picture Library, pages 117, 127 (below), 128 (above); The Museum of London, page 6; Trustees of the National Library of Scotland, page 37; Norfolk Library and Information Service, page 126; Christopher Pinney/National Portrait Gallery, page 65; Private Collection, England/National Portrait Gallery, London, pages 76, 78; Robert Opie, pages 63; Popperfoto, page 59; 'By Courtesy of the Post Office', page 31; Punch, pages 86, 102; The Royal Archives © Her Majesty Queen Elizabeth II, page 92; The Royal Collection © 1993, Her Majesty Queen Elizabeth II, page 22 (below); Trustees of the Science Museum, pages 12, 36, 38, 39, 40; © 'Courtesy of Sheffield City Museum', page 17; Topham Picture Source, page 35; Masters and Fellows of Trinity College, Cambridge, page 105; 'The Stonepickers', Laing Art Gallery, Newcastle upon Tyne (Tyne and Wear Museums), page 104 (below); 'By Courtesy of the Trustees of the Wedgwood Museum, Barlaston, Stoke-on-Trent, Staffordshire, England', page 118; Weidenfeld and Nicolson Archives, page 104 (above); Welsh History Resources Unit, page 114; Woodmansterne/Castle Museum, York, pages 43, 48.

Cover photograph: National Trust Photographic Library
Picture research: Sandie Huskinson-Rolfe (PHOTOSEEKERS)

Pearson Education Limited
*Edinburgh Gate, Harlow, Essex, CM20 2JE, England
and Associated Companies throughout the World.*

© Longman Group UK Limited 1993

First published 1993
Ninth impression 2005
ISBN-10: 0-582-20738-X
ISBN-13: 978-0-582-20738-7

*Typeset in Monotype Lasercomp 12/14 Photina
Printed in China*
GCC/09

*The publisher's policy is to use paper manufactured
from sustainable forests*

*Designed by Michael Harris
Illustrated by Tony Richardson (The Wooden Ark Studio)
and Kathy Baxendale*

Contents

1
The Crystal Palace

'One of the wonders of the world'

On the morning of 1 May 1851 thousands of people made their way through the streets of London to Hyde Park. They were heading for the city's newest building, the Crystal Palace (source 1). It was designed and built especially to hold what the organisers called an 'Exhibition of the Works of **Industry** of all Nations', known ever since as the Great Exhibition. The crowds had come to see the opening of the exhibition by Queen Victoria and her husband, Prince Albert.

No one had seen anything quite like the Crystal Palace before. People expected large buildings to be made of bricks and stone. The Crystal Palace was made of iron and glass. 'One of the wonders of the world', Queen Victoria called it in her journal. She said the sun shining in through the high glass roof gave the inside 'a fairy-like appearance'.

SOURCE 1

The Crystal Palace in Hyde Park. A writer in the magazine *Punch* nicknamed the building 'Crystal Palace' and the name stuck.

It was all built so quickly (nine months from the builders taking over the site to the last painter leaving), and the result seemed so magical, that one poet said it was as if a wizard waved his wand and:

SOURCE 2

A blazing arch of lucid [shining] glass
Leaps like a fountain from the grass
To meet the sun!

Thackeray, 'May Day Ode', 1851

The 'wizard' who designed the Crystal Palace was Joseph Paxton, the manager of the Duke of Devonshire's estates. He based the design on a conservatory he had built for the Duke at his family home, Chatsworth.

His design used the very latest technology. The Crystal Palace could not have been built fifty years before. It was built of interchangeable parts (source 3). The iron girders, columns and gutters were all identical. The machines that made the various parts to exactly the same sizes had only recently been invented.

SOURCE 3

Building the Crystal Palace. This picture shows one of the semi-circular ribs for the roof of the central section being lifted into place. Two thousand workers handled 3,900 tonnes of ironwork, raised 2,300 girders and 3,300 pillars into position, fixed 48 kilometres of guttering and fitted over 300,000 metres of glass.

The Great Exhibition

SOURCE 4

The inside of the Crystal Palace. It was 563 metres long, 124 metres wide and 20 metres high, except in the central section (shown here) where it rose to 33 metres and enclosed several of the elm trees growing in Hyde Park. Exhibits were shown on the floor area and in the galleries above.

Inside the Crystal Palace were thousands of objects sent to the Great Exhibition from all over the world (source 4). One half of the space was allocated to exhibits from Great Britain and her colonies. The colonies were lands occupied and ruled by the British. They included the Caribbean islands known as the British West Indies, Canada, Australia, parts of South Africa and India. Together the colonies made up the British Empire which had expanded rapidly in the eighteenth century from its small beginnings in the sixteenth.

Foreign countries occupied the rest of the space. France and Germany provided the largest displays; China was represented; so was the United States of America which sent its latest inventions: Colt's revolver, McCormick's mechanical reaper and several sewing machines.

The objects on display included works of art, hand-made goods such as lace and pottery, raw materials such as coal and machine-made products such as **textiles**.

> **i** **Textiles**   Cloth that is made by weaving. The name is also used for materials that can be spun and woven into cloth, such as wool, flax, cotton and silk.

SOURCE 5

The Machinery Court at the Great Exhibition.

activity

I What can you learn from sources 3 and 5 about British industry in about 1850?

It was the machines themselves which fascinated the crowds most of all (source 5). *The Times* newspaper declared the exhibits to be:

SOURCE 6

All that is useful and beautiful in nature, art and science.

The Times, 2 May 1851

This would have pleased Prince Albert. The idea of holding the Exhibition was partly his, and he led the committee which organised it. He believed it was possible for things to be both useful and beautiful, and he wanted to bring art and mechanical skills together. Above all, he believed people were living through a time of wonderful change brought about by modern inventions which were improving everyone's life. He believed that all countries of the world were part of this process and that it would unite them together in peace. The aim of the Great Exhibition, he said:

SOURCE 7

Is to give us . . . a living picture of the point of development at which the whole of mankind has arrived . . . and a new starting-point from which all nations will be able to direct their exertions [efforts].

Prince Albert, Speech in Manchester, 21 March 1850

The visitors

SOURCE 8

'Agriculturalists at the Exhibition', a drawing from the *Illustrated London News*, 1851. Many landlords and factory owners paid for their workers to travel to London and see the Great Exhibition.

Over six million people visited the Great Exhibition in just over five months. Of these, just under four and a half million were people who went on Mondays to Thursdays, which were the cheap '**shilling** [5p] days'. For many it was their first trip to London (source 8). They were able to get there from all over Britain thanks to another recent invention, the railway:

SOURCE 9

> *The first real event of my life came in 1851, when I was six years old. My mother then took me up to town to see the Great Exhibition. Our special Exhibition train from Thirsk to King's Cross was a wonder to me . . . The train was of enormous length and drawn by six locomotives.*
>
> R. E. Crompton, *Reminiscences*, 1928

Some feared the large crowds of working people would cause trouble. They did not. The extra policemen drafted in for shilling days were not needed. People wanted to learn:

SOURCE 10

> *Whether it be . . . the splashing centrifugal pump . . . or the bewildering whirl of the cylindrical steam press – round each and all . . . are . . . farmers, and servants, and youths, and children clustered, endeavouring to solve the mystery of the complex operations.*
>
> Henry Mayhew, *'1851'*, 1851

> **ℹ Shilling** Since 1972 we have used a decimal coinage in the UK. Before that, 12 pennies (12d) made 1 shilling (1s) and 20s made £1 (100p). The skilled workers who built the Crystal Palace earned 28s (£1.40) a week on average. Visitors to the Great Exhibition could buy a plate of ham for 6d (2.5p).

The Crystal Palace

SOURCE 11

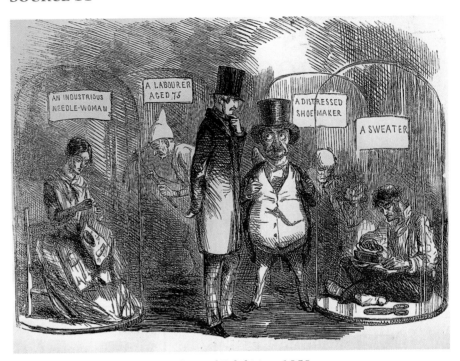

Specimens from Mr Punch's Industrial Exhibition, 1850.

activity

1 In what ways do sources 8, 9 and 10 suggest that The Great Exhibition mattered to people
a all over Britain
b from different social backgrounds?
2 Use the sources and information in Part 1 to make a list of the things which you think might have most impressed a visitor to the Great Exhibition.
3 Write a short newspaper article describing the Great Exhibition from the point of view of the person who drew source 11.

The Great Exhibition was the talking point of 1851 for people of all backgrounds all over Britain. It caused them to stop for a moment and think about the changes that were going on around them.

A hundred years before, towns were small and railways unheard of. There were only a few machines, mostly driven by wind, water or horsepower, and no factories. Looking at the Crystal Palace, people realised it could not have been built even fifty years before, as the machines which made it possible had not been invented then.

In many ways the Crystal Palace stood for their hopes and dreams. It combined the latest technology with a beauty of design. The exhibition inside showed that British manufactures were the best in the world. New inventions were appearing every day.

Many people felt that Prince Albert was right. Led by Britain, the people of the world had the ability to make useful and beautiful things which would give them happier and more comfortable lives. Looking ahead, they hoped for peace, prosperity and progress.

The year before, however, a cartoon in the magazine *Punch* had pointed out that things were not as simple as that (source 11). Mr Punch's 'Industrial Exhibition' showed some of those who were not benefiting at all from Britain's prosperity and progress. For them the Crystal Palace might as well have been in fairyland, where Queen Victoria so often pictured it.

2 Great Changes 1750–1900

Three great changes

More changes took place in Britain between 1750 and 1900 than in any period other than the twentieth century. A person living in 1750 might have gone back in time to the Middle Ages and felt quite at home. Someone going back in time from 1900 to the Middle Ages would have felt a complete stranger. Part Two is about three of the great changes that happened between 1750 and 1900 and the effect they had on the lives of the British people.

Population and cities

SOURCE 1

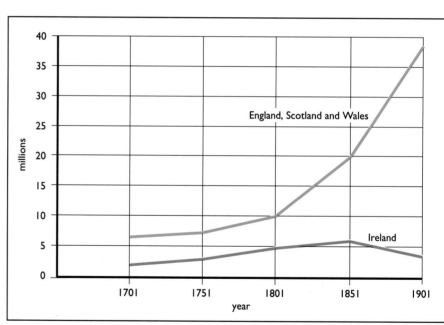

Population change in England, Wales, Scotland and Ireland, 1701–1901. The first official population count, or census, took place in 1801 and has been repeated every ten years since then, except in 1941 because of the Second World War. Historians have to estimate eighteenth-century population figures using information from parish registers.

Between 1750 and 1900 the number of people in Britain increased more than three times (source 1). There were also changes in the numbers of people living in various parts of the country (sources 2a, b, c). These changes were caused partly by the overall increase in population and partly by people moving from one area to another.

activity

1 Look at source 2. Between 1801 and 1911, in which parts of Britain did population density
a increase the most?
b stay the same?
2 What reasons can you think of for this?

SOURCE 2a

SOURCE 2b

SOURCE 2c

KEY

persons per square kilometre (km²)

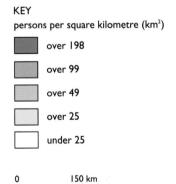

over 198

over 99

over 49

over 25

under 25

0   150 km

Population density. These maps show the number of people
per square kilometre of land in 1801, 1851 and 1911.

One of the most dramatic changes in the nineteenth century was the increase in the proportion of the population living in towns rather than in the countryside (source 3). Another was the rate at which the population of the new industrial cities grew, especially between 1801 and 1851. Bradford grew from 13,000 inhabitants in 1801 to 104,000 in 1851; Leeds from 53,000 to 172,000. Manchester had a population of 95,000 in 1801, 303,000 in 1851 and 654,000 in 1901.

SOURCE 3

The percentage numbers of people living in towns and in the countryside, 1801–1901.

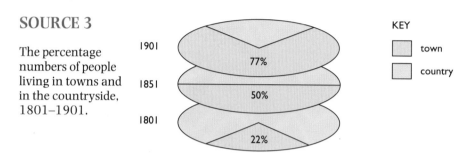

1901   77%

1851   50%

1801   22%

KEY

☐ town

☐ country

Railways

SOURCE 4

The opening of Scotland's first passenger train service, the Glasgow to Garnkirk line, in 1831. In the early trains passengers travelling first class went in closed carriages. Those travelling second and third class had to make do with open trucks.

The first passenger railway, the Liverpool and Manchester, opened in 1829. The first in Scotland (source 4), followed two years later.

By the early 1840s there were about 2,000 miles of track in use. By 1855 more than 8,000 miles of track linked all the major cities of Britain. By 1870 the network covered the entire country (source 5).

SOURCE 5

The growth of the railway network, 1840–70.

SOURCE 6

'The Railway Station', painted by **W. P. Frith** in 1862. The station is Paddington in London. Find:
● The locomotive
● Porters putting luggage on the carriage roofs
● Policemen arresting a wanted man (far right)
● What other incidents can you see?

Many different companies built and ran railways. People called shareholders put up the money for a company to build track, locomotives, carriages and buildings. Once the company started to make money, the shareholders were paid a share of the profits.

To begin with only the better-off could afford to travel by train. In 1844 Parliament passed a law stating that each railway company had to run at least one train every weekday at a fare of not more than one penny (0.4p) a mile for adults and a halfpenny for children. This opened up travel by train to everyone. In the 1840s people thought of it as new and exciting. By the 1860s they took it for granted and many people used the railways (source 6).

activity

Work in pairs.
1 Look at sources 4 and 6. What do they suggest were
a the similarities
b the differences
in railway travel beween 1831 and 1862?
2 How do source 6 and sources 1 and 4 in Part 1 suggest that the Crystal Palace might have influenced the architecture of other buildings?

i **W. P. Frith** William Powell Frith (1819–1909) was famous for his paintings of life in the mid-nineteenth century. In paintings such as 'Ramsgate Sands', 1851 (source 22, page 22), 'Derby Day', 1858 and 'The Railway Station', 1862 he tried to show many different sorts of people and incidents in realistic detail.

Factories

In 1750 most **manufactures** were made in people's homes. The system was called the 'domestic' or 'putting-out' system (source 7). Textiles (source 8), lace, chains and nails were all made by putting-out.

> **Manufactures** originally meant things made by hand (from the Latin words 'manu' meaning 'by hand' and 'factum' meaning 'made'). Around 1600 it also came to mean things made by physical labour helped by machines. The workshops where things were made, especially on a large scale, came to be known as 'manufactories' or 'factories'. 'Manufacturer' can mean either the owner of a factory or a worker in a factory.

> **Capital**　*Money that can be used to start up a business.*

SOURCE 7

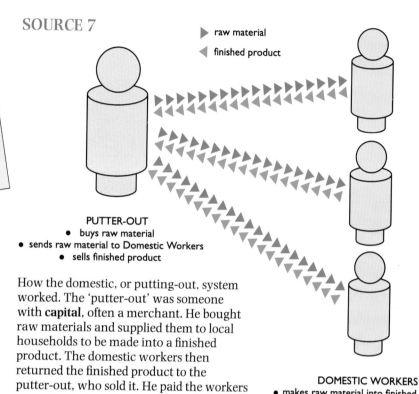

▶ raw material

◀ finished product

PUTTER-OUT
- buys raw material
- sends raw material to Domestic Workers
- sells finished product

DOMESTIC WORKERS
- makes raw material into finished product
- returns finished product to Putter-Out

How the domestic, or putting-out, system worked. The 'putter-out' was someone with **capital**, often a merchant. He bought raw materials and supplied them to local households to be made into a finished product. The domestic workers then returned the finished product to the putter-out, who sold it. He paid the workers according to how much they produced.

SOURCE 8

A framework knitter and his family working at home in 1751. Framework knitters lived in the villages of the east midlands and made men's 'hose', or stockings, and waistcoats.

SOURCE 9

The inside of Marshall's flax-spinning mill, opened in 1840. It was equipped with steam-driven spinning machines.

By 1900 most manufactures were made in factories (source 9).
Goods were mass produced. That is, things were made in great
numbers with the help of machines which could turn out identical
parts. Workers either ran the machines or assembled the various
parts the machines produced.

Factories were first set up by cotton manufacturers in the late
eighteenth century. The machines were driven by water power, so
the factories were built beside rivers in the hills of Derbyshire and
Lancashire. In about 1800 the manufacturers started to use
steam-powered machines. Steam engines ran on coal and so new
factories were built in towns near coal fields where there were also
people to work in them. There were no cotton spinning mills in
Manchester in 1773; in 1802 there were fifty-two.

Even so, the factory system did not suddenly take over. By 1850
about half of all manufacturing workers were in factories.
Manufacturing workers formed less than a quarter of the whole
working population, so there were many people who did not work
in factories.

activity

Work in pairs.
1 Look at source 9.
a What impression of
working conditions does it
give you?
b What aspects of working
conditions cannot be
expressed in a picture?
2 Look at sources 8 and 9.
How many differences can
you think of between
working in the putting-out
system and working in the
factory system?

The impact of the changes

The rise in population, the growth of cities, the invention and development of railways, and the introduction of factories – between them, these changes altered the lives of the British people almost beyond recognition.

Industrial cities

The growth of cities in the first half of the nineteenth century created new problems for their inhabitants (source 10). Thousands of people suddenly found themselves crowded together in one place. Smoke from factories polluted the air. Builders made quick profits by throwing up cheap, badly built houses in terraces which often shared a back wall. These back-to-back houses (source 11) were only one room deep so the light could get in. Because they had no back doors or back windows, they were very badly ventilated.

SOURCE 11

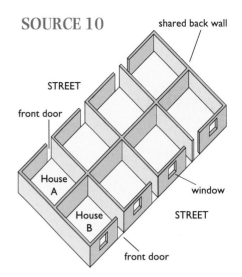

SOURCE 10

Back-to-back houses.

activity

3 Look at source 11.
a What possible links does it suggest between the growth of Sheffield and (i) the river, (ii) the railway?
b What does it tell you about living conditions in Sheffield?

Sheffield in about 1850, painted by William Ibbit.

activity

1 Use the sources and information on pages 17–18. What effects did the growth of industrial cities have on the home lives of the people living in them?

In the 1860s a Frenchman visiting Manchester wrote:

SOURCE 12

What dreary streets. Through half-open windows we could see the wretched rooms at ground level, or often below the earth's damp surface. Masses of . . . children, dirty and flabby of flesh, crowd each threshold and breath the vile air of the street, less vile than that within.

Hippolyte Taine, *Notes on England*, written in the 1860s

The houses had no proper water supply and no drainage. The lavatory was usually a pit in a shed shared with other families. Rubbish was never cleared. The Medical Officer of Health said the houses at Greenhill in Swansea had:

SOURCE 13

No cleanliness within, and no drainage without: stagnant water soaking through the walls, with no place to discharge itself . . . the floors in many cases . . . unbricked and in wet weather becoming a mass of mud . . . the garden . . . heaped with ashes, and in many cases stored with pig dung.

Report of the Swansea Medical Officer of Health, 1853

In these conditions diseases such as cholera and typhus flourished. The death rate in the cities was far higher than in the countryside. In 1842, for example, the death rate for Wales as a whole was 2 per cent, but in Cardiff it was 3 per cent.

In the second half of the nineteenth century living conditions in cities improved. Town councils laid on water supplies and built sewers. They lit streets by gas and created parks. Even so, many of the very poor continued to live in dirty, overcrowded houses in dingy streets and courtyards near city centres.

New types of work

The railways created new jobs and destroyed some old ones (source 14). Some of the new jobs were very skilled. Train drivers and guards, for example, were well paid and lived quite comfortable lives compared with other workers.

Other jobs were less well paid but brought new opportunities to unexpected places such as Wolverton in Buckinghamshire. There the London and North Western Railway Company chose to build a refreshment stop (when trains had no corridors, passengers needed frequent stops on long journeys). A staff of 28, including cooks, bakers, waiters, waitresses and housemaids, served passengers from 7.30 in the morning to 11 o'clock at night.

The building of the railways also gave work to thousands of men known as 'navvies' (source 15). 'Navvy' came from 'navigator', the name given in the eighteenth century to labourers employed to dig canals. In 1845 there were about 200,000 navvies working on 3,000 miles (4,828 kilometres) of new line.

activity

2 Look at source 14.
a What form of transport was ended by the coming of the railways?
b Whose jobs do you think were destroyed as a result?
c What opinions about the coming of the railways do you think might be held by (i) the driver of the coach, (ii) the drivers of the two trains, (iii) the passengers? Explain your answers in as much detail as you can.

SOURCE 14

'Past and Present', engraved by the Leighton brothers.

SOURCE 15

Navvies at work. This picture, from a report on safety published in 1840, illustrates the various dangers faced by navvies. Many navvies came from Scotland, Ireland and the Lancashire and Yorkshire dales. They worked in gangs and lived in camps near their work.

Like the railways, the factory system created new skilled jobs. For example, engineers were needed to build the machines that factories used. The new unskilled jobs involved the routine work of running the machines.

Mass production in factories also destroyed jobs, many of them in the countryside. Between 1871 and 1901, the number of village tailors and shoemakers fell by as much as a half in many areas. The number of women lacemakers in Berkshire fell from 8,077 to 789. The number of women straw plaiters who made hats and bonnets in Bedfordshire (see source 4, Part 8) fell from 20,701 in 1871 to 485 in 1901.

The demand for village craftspeople fell, too. Farmers saw many more advertisements such as this one from a Wolverhampton firm:

SOURCE 16

Cattle Hurdles five bars from 39s 6d per dozen, delivered free . . . Specially low prices quoted . . . for all kinds of fencing, Hurdles, . . . Gates . . . Tanks, Troughs, etc.

Quoted in P. Horn, *The Changing Countryside in Victorian and Edwardian England and Wales*, 1984

It was cheaper for them to buy mass-produced carts, ladders, buckets and hayrakes than those made by traditional carpenters and wheelwrights.

Ploughs and metal tools, and agricultural machines such as threshers (source 17) and reapers were made in towns by big new firms such as Taskers of Andover in Hampshire and Ransomes of Ipswich in Suffolk. All this took away work traditionally done by village blacksmiths.

The growth of manufacturing industry and towns meant an increase in businesses of all kinds. Banks, insurance companies, the factories and railway companies all needed clerks to do office work.

SOURCE 17

A steam thresher. At least two third of the corn produced in England wa: being steam threshed by 1890.

---

activity

1 When complete, this chart will show which jobs were lost, and which created, as a result of the great changes between 1750 and 1900. It also shows whether a job was skilled or unskilled.
a Copy it out.
b Use the sources and information on pages 18–21 to help you to fill it in. Do this in as much detail as you can.
2 Use the sources and information on pages 17–20. What impact did the growth of towns and the development of railways have on jobs in the countryside?

Jobs Lost	Unskilled	Skilled	Jobs Gained	Unskilled	Skilled
Coach drivers		✓	Train drivers		✓
Blacksmiths		✓	Navvies	✓	
Straw plaiters	✓		Domestic servants	✓	

An increasing number of families wished to employ servants, particularly women, in their houses. In 1851 there were over one million female domestic servants; by 1901 there were two million. These women came from country districts or were the daughters of working families in towns. Many of them left service to get married.

Leisure and entertainment

In the eighteenth century, people worked long hours on the land or making things at home. Sundays, saints' days and local festival days provided occasions for them to take part in various traditional sports and pastimes. In the nineteenth century, factory owners wanted a disciplined and reliable work force, not one that kept on taking frequent breaks from work on 'holy days'.

Slowly the old ways died out and a new pattern developed. Sundays remained a day off. In 1850 textile workers were also granted a half-day off on Saturdays. In the second half of the century this spread to other workers, too. In 1871 the Bank Holiday Act created four official holidays a year: Christmas, Easter, Whitsuntide and the last Monday in August. Even so, workers were not always paid for them.

Traditional sports and pastimes were often violent and brutal. In 1849 William Lovett told an enquiry he thought working people were less interested in them than they had been when he first arrived in London in 1828:

SOURCE 18

At that period [1828] you might see the working classes of London flocking out into the fields on a Sunday morning, or during a holiday . . . deciding their contests and challenges by pugilistic combats [fist fights]. It was no uncommon thing . . . on taking a Sunday morning's walk, to see about twenty such fights. Dog fights and cock fights were equally common.

Evidence to the Select Committee on Public Libraries, 1849

Even so, cruel sports such as cock-fighting survived well into the 1860s and crowds flocked to see the last public hanging in 1864.

Fairs, another traditional entertainment, also remained popular:

SOURCE 19

*What a delightful racket there is as you gaze round the sea of faces and listen to the bands of the various shows . . . There is the clanging of cymbals, the firing of guns, the cracking of whips and the distant roar of the wild animals in the far-famed Wombell's **Menagerie**.*

Louis M. Hayes, *Reminiscences of Manchester and Some of Its Local Surroundings from the Year 1840*, written in 1905

activity

3 Look at sources 18–21 and the information in the text.
a Describe the ways in which the use of leisure time by working people living in towns changed during the nineteenth century.
b Do you think each change happened quickly or slowly? Give your reasons.
4 In what ways do sources 19–21 suggest that city life in the nineteenth century had its good points?

i **Menagerie**   A collection of wild animals kept in cages.

The public house, or pub, provided the most popular social centre for most working people in both town and country, much to the annoyance of reformers who disapproved of drink and wanted them to pass their leisure time more usefully. From the 1870s theatres and music halls (source 20) became their favourite places of entertainment in the cities, especially London. This is how one writer remembered the music hall of the early 1900s:

SOURCE 21

If Mum could afford it we had a bag of peanuts or a ha'penny bag of sweets. We went in the 'gallery' for twopence – half-price for us kids . . . Among the dramas I remember was The Face at the Window *– real horrible. Others were* Sweeney Todd, Maria Marten *. . . Sometimes we went to Collins Music Hall or the Islington Empire . . . They always had variety shows.*

A. S. Jasper, *A Hoxton Childhood*, written in the 1970s

The railways probably made the most difference to the way people spent their leisure time. Between 1842 and 1848 the number of passengers who travelled on the railways of the United Kingdom rose from 64,000 a year to 174,000. The number who travelled at the cheapest rate (third class) rose from 19,000 to 86,000.

SOURCE 20

Saturday night out at the music hall, 1872.

SOURCE 22

'Ramsgate Sands', 1854, painted by W. P. Frith.

activity

1a Look at sources 22–23 and the information in the text. How did the railways change people's use of leisure time?
b Look at source 23. How did the railways affect people's knowledge and experience?

In 1841, Thomas Cook, founder of the famous travel agency, organised the first cheap day excursion from Leicester to Loughborough. After that, trips to London or the seaside became common (source 22). Thanks to these, said one writer:

SOURCE 23

The 'people' . . . have been enabled . . . to . . . travel to distances which their forefathers had neither time nor money to undertake. The working class of 30, or even 15, years ago did not know their own country. Very few travelled for pleasure beyond a small circle around the place which they inhabited.

The Illustrated London News, September 1850

assignments

1 Use the sources and information in Part 2.
a Give a talk or make a display to describe some of the main differences in the way of life of British people in 1750 and in 1900.
b Make a chart or diagram to show the various links between (i) the growth of cities, (ii) the development of railways, (iii) the development of the factory system.

2 Choose
either the growth of population (pages 10–12)
   or the development of railways (pages 12–14)
   or the development of the factory system (pages 15–16).
Decide whether you think the change took place rapidly or gradually. Write a paragraph giving your reasons.

3 Look at the information about the London and North Western Railway's refreshment stop at Wolverton on page 18. Wolverton was a country village.
a Where might the people who worked at the refreshment stop have worked before it was built?
b Apart from creating new jobs, how else do you think the refreshment stop effected the area?
c Which local people might have been (i) pleased, (ii) annoyed that it had been built?
d What other changes – suggested by the sources and information in Part 2 – might a country village have seen in the nineteenth century? Give the reasons for all your answers in as much detail as you can.

3 The Industrial Revolution

What was the Industrial Revolution?

Between 1750 and 1900 Britain was transformed. In 1750 it was a mainly agricultural country with a small population. Towns were small. There were some manufacturers, miners and merchants; but the great majority of people lived by farming. For many of them the threat of starvation through harvest failure was never far away. Few lived in any great comfort.

In 1900 Britain depended on the mass production of goods in factories and on the mining and processing of raw materials such as coal and iron (source 1). There was a large population. Many people lived in big towns and cities. Those who earned their living by farming were now a minority. The threat of starvation was very slight. A large number of people lived in reasonable comfort.

The 'Industrial Revolution' is the name given to the changes which caused this transformation. Historians disagree about exactly when it began and when it can be said to have ended. Nevertheless, most agree that the really big changes took place between about 1750 and 1850.

SOURCE 1

Cyfartha Ironworks in South Wales.

The cotton textile industry was the first to move into mass production by machines in factories. The amount produced, or output, doubled every ten years from the 1780s to the 1850s (source 2a). There was a similar massive rise in the production of coal and **pig-iron** (sources 2b and 2c).

i Pig-iron The name given to iron which has been made from iron ore in a blast furnace. It can be re-melted and poured into moulds to make cast-iron.

SOURCE 2

The rise in production of cotton textiles, coal and pig-iron.

SOURCE 2a

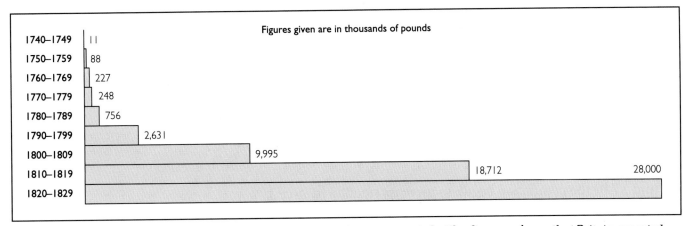

Figures given are in thousands of pounds

Period	Value
1740–1749	11
1750–1759	88
1760–1769	227
1770–1779	248
1780–1789	756
1790–1799	2,631
1800–1809	9,995
1810–1819	18,712
1820–1829	28,000

Exports of cotton textiles, measured in thousands of pounds and ten-year periods. The diagram shows that Britain exported £11,000 worth of cotton textiles in the period 1740–49 and £28,000,000 worth in 1820–29.

SOURCE 2b

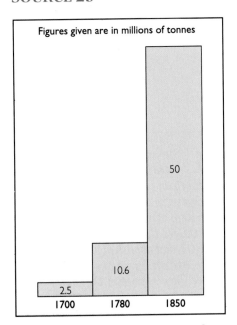

Figures given are in millions of tonnes

50

10.6

2.5

1700   1780   1850

Coal output in millions of tonnes. The diagram shows that coal output rose by 8.1 million tonnes in the eighty years from 1700 to 1780, and by 34.4 million tonnes in the seventy years from 1780 to 1850.

SOURCE 2c

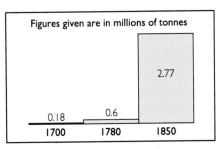

Figures given are in millions of tonnes

2.77

0.18   0.6

1700   1780   1850

Pig-iron output in millions of tonnes. The diagram shows that pig-iron output rose from 180,000 tonnes in 1700 to 2,770,000 tonnes in 1850.

activity

1 Look at sources 2a, 2b and 2c.
a How do they tell you that the production of (i) cotton textiles, (ii) coal, (iii) pig-iron began to increase more rapidly after about 1780 than before?
b How do these sources and the information on these two pages suggest that, even so, the Industrial Revolution took place quite slowly?
2 'Industrial' means to do with industry and 'revolution' means a very big change indeed. Do you think 'Industrial Revolution' is a good description of what happened in Britain between about 1750 and 1850?

Why did the Industrial Revolution happen?

Britain was the first country in the world to have an industrial revolution and historians are still not clear exactly why it happened when it did. There appear to have been many different factors, or influences, at work. Each played its part but would have been unable to make the changes happen on its own. The rest of this section is about five of these factors – population, trade, agriculture, transport and inventions – and how each one helped to make the Industrial Revolution possible.

Population

Around 1740 the population began to increase steadily (source 1, page 10). First there was a fall in the death rate because for the first time there were no major epidemics such as the plague. Then there was a rise in the birth rate.

This is how the rise in population helped to make the Industrial Revolution possible:

- It meant there were more people wanting to buy goods. This is called an increase in 'demand'. When demand rises the prices of goods go up because there are more people trying to buy things than there are things to go round. When prices go up manufacturers try to make more goods so they can make bigger profits. So eighteenth-century manufacturers decided it was worth spending money on new machinery and factories to enable them to produce more goods more cheaply.
- It meant more people were available to work. So when manufacturers needed workers there were people willing to go into factories.

Trade

Merchants make a living out of buying and selling. In particular they try to buy things cheaply in one place and move them to another where they can sell them at a profit. Very often this involves shipping raw materials from one part of the world to another where they can be turned into a finished product.

i **Invest** *To use money to buy something which is expected to make a profit, or to lend it in return for interest.*

i **Slaves** *African slaves were first taken to the American colonies in 1619. They were traded as if they were an item of goods. Britain outlawed the slave trade in 1807 and abolished slavery in the British Empire in 1833 (see Part 9, pages 116–119).*

i **Calico** *Cotton cloth. So called because it originally came from Calicut on the east coast of India.*

SOURCE 3

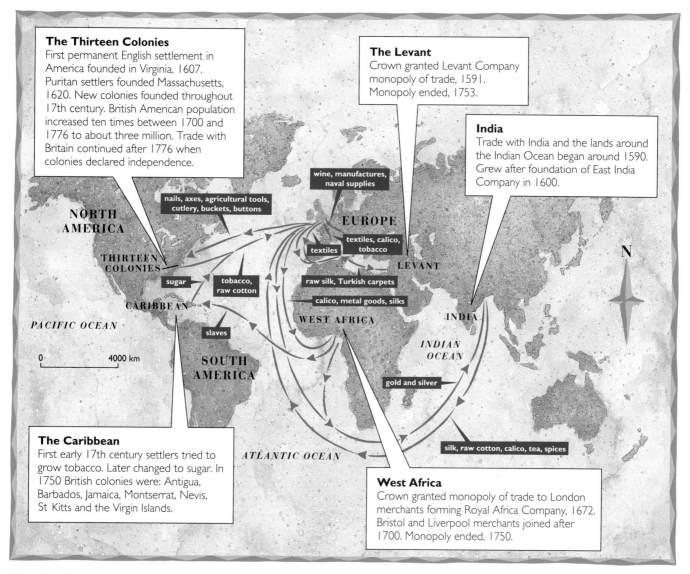

The Thirteen Colonies
First permanent English settlement in America founded in Virginia, 1607. Puritan settlers founded Massachusetts, 1620. New colonies founded throughout 17th century. British American population increased ten times between 1700 and 1776 to about three million. Trade with Britain continued after 1776 when colonies declared independence.

The Levant
Crown granted Levant Company monopoly of trade, 1591. Monopoly ended, 1753.

India
Trade with India and the lands around the Indian Ocean began around 1590. Grew after foundation of East India Company in 1600.

The Caribbean
First early 17th century settlers tried to grow tobacco. Later changed to sugar. In 1750 British colonies were: Antigua, Barbados, Jamaica, Montserrat, Nevis, St Kitts and the Virgin Islands.

West Africa
Crown granted monopoly of trade to London merchants forming Royal Africa Company, 1672. Bristol and Liverpool merchants joined after 1700. Monopoly ended, 1750.

Map labels: wine, manufactures, naval supplies · nails, axes, agricultural tools, cutlery, buckets, buttons · textiles, calico, tobacco · textiles · sugar · tobacco, raw cotton · raw silk, Turkish carpets · calico, metal goods, silks · slaves · gold and silver · silk, raw cotton, calico, tea, spices

Map regions: NORTH AMERICA · THIRTEEN COLONIES · CARIBBEAN · PACIFIC OCEAN · SOUTH AMERICA · ATLANTIC OCEAN · EUROPE · LEVANT · WEST AFRICA · INDIA · INDIAN OCEAN · 0 — 4000 km · N

British trade in 1750. British merchants shipped manufactured goods to West Africa and exchanged them for **slaves**, gold and ivory. They shipped the slaves to the Caribbean and the American colonies to work on tobacco, sugar and cotton plantations. There they sold them for sugar, tobacco and raw cotton which they shipped back to Britain. The gold and ivory was shipped to India in return for tea, coffee, spices, **calico** and raw cotton. Merchants then sent much of the tea, coffee, spices, sugar and tobacco to Europe in return for essential goods such as wood, hemp and tar which were needed to build and repair ships. They also exported woollen goods to Europe which was the largest market of all for British goods.

In 1750 British merchants were at the centre of a very prosperous world-wide trading network (source 3). Trade helped to make the Industrial Revolution possible because it:

- Made some merchants rich enough to have spare capital to **invest** in the new manufacturing businesses.
- Provided markets abroad as well as at home for the new cotton goods. This added to the demand for them. In 1750 cotton goods were only 1 per cent of all Britain's exports. In 1800 they were 39 per cent.
- Provided the raw material, raw cotton, for the manufacture of these goods.

activity

1 How was demand increased by
a the rise in population
b trade?
2 Explain the connections between trade and manufacturing.

Agriculture

In 1800 a British farmer could grow about one third more corn on a piece of land than could be grown on it in 1700. The main reason for this was that during the eighteenth century farmers began to use a new system of crop growing that had become popular in East Anglia in the seventeenth century (source 4).

SOURCE 4

activity

I The open-field system required farmers to cooperate very closely.
a Why do you think that was?
b Why do you think it held up the introduction of new methods?

Year	Crop	Notes
I	Wheat	Takes goodness out of soil.
2	Turnips	Feed animals in winter. Enrich soil.
	Sheep	Eat turnips. Manure soil with dung.
3	Barley	Needs rich soil. Removes goodness.
4	Clover	Enriches soil again. Feeds animals in winter.
	Cows	Eat clover. Manure soil with dung.
		Plough. Then plant wheat for repeat of year I.

The new system of crop growing. The traditional method was to grow crops on a field for two years and then leave it uncultivated, or fallow, for the third year so that the goodness could return to the soil. With the new method farmers planted turnips or clover instead of letting a field lie fallow.

The increase in food production was also helped by enclosure (source 5). This involved taking the old open fields, in which farmers held strips of land to farm, and dividing them up into several smaller fields, each surrounded by its own fence or hedge. Farmers then owned or rented individual fields. This made it much easier for them to introduce new farming methods.

SOURCE 5

Surveyors preparing land for enclosure at Henlow in Bedfordshire. They had to decide how to parcel out the open fields among the owners of the strips. Common land was often enclosed too. In 1700 about 70 per cent of all land in England was enclosed. By 1830 the figure was about 90 per cent.

SOURCE 6

Thomas Coke (1750–1842) inspecting his sheep on his estate at Holkham in Norfolk. Coke did not invent the new farming methods, but he helped to advertise them by running a model farm and holding agricultural shows. They spread among country gentlemen with medium to large landholdings and farmers renting farms.

activity

2 What were the connections between agricultural improvements and
a the rise in population
b factories
c capital
d transport?

i Agricultural machines Jethro Tull invented a horse hoe and seed drill which sowed seeds in rows instead of scattering them wastefully. He wrote a book, Horse Hoeing Husbandry (1731), but his methods were not much used in the eighteenth century. Andrew Meikle invented a mechanical thresher (1786), and Ransome of Ipswich an improved plough (1780).

Other farming developments in the mid-eighteenth century included experiments in breeding fatter sheep and cattle which would provide more meat (source 6), and the invention of some early **agricultural machines**. The breeding experiments led to a gradual improvement in food production but the inventions made very little difference because they were not widely used until the nineteenth century.

This is how changes in agriculture helped to make the Industrial Revolution possible:

- The extra food farmers produced fed the growing population. The population could only go up if there was enough food for more people.
- The extra food was produced without needing to use more farm workers. So the extra numbers in the population were free to work in mines and factories, where more workers were needed.
- By about 1800 the price of food started to fall because farmers were producing plenty of it. This meant people could spend less money on food and have a bit more to spend on manufactures.
- The profit from higher rents and the sale of more crops and animals made landowners wealthier. Many of them used their spare money to improve roads and canals (see pages 30–32) and to invest in industry.

Transport

Between about 1660 and 1750 it became much easier to transport things around Britain. Rivers were improved so that boats and barges could sail much further along them. The surfaces of many roads were improved by turnpike trusts.

These were groups of local people (called 'trustees') who were given permission by Parliament to look after a stretch of road. They took over from the parishes through which the road ran. In return, those who used the road had to pay a fee or toll (source 7). The trustees were not allowed to make a profit. They had to use all the money to improve the road. To do that, they employed surveyors and engineers.

The number of turnpike roads in England and Wales rose from 250 in 1760 to 1,116 in the 1830s. Better road surfaces meant that carriers could use wagons instead of packhorses to transport goods.

SOURCE 7

Toll charges on the London–Holyhead road.

activity

1 Look at source 7 and the information in the text.

a Many parishes had not kept their roads in good repair. Why do you think that was?

b What reasons might people have for setting up a turnpike trust?

c Which members of a parish do you think were most likely to object to paying the new tolls?

d Why do you think vehicles with narrow wheels or with nails sticking out of their wheels had to pay a higher toll?

SOURCE 8

The Edinburgh mail passing the Stamford Hill turnpike just before dawn on the last stage of its journey to the General Post Office in London. It covered about 400 miles (644 kilometres) in just over 40 hours. Allowing for stops, this meant an average speed of about 11 m.p.h. (18 km.p.h.). By law mail coaches did not pay tolls.

> **ℹ Thomas Telford**
> *Thomas Telford (1757–1834), the son of a Scottish shepherd, became an architect and civil engineer. In 1815 he was commissioned to build a fast coaching road (today's A5) from London to Holyhead, the port used by Irish MPs after the union of Ireland and England in 1801. He also designed the suspension bridge over the Menai Straits. His work cut the journey from 42 to less than 27 hours.*

> **ℹ John McAdam** *John McAdam (1756–1836) was a Scot who emigrated to America. He returned in 1783 and started to investigate methods of building and repairing roads. He invented a popular and cheap system using small broken stones.*

They also encouraged people to start to travel by stage-coach. In the 1780s the Post Office started to use coaches for its mail services (source 8).

In the early nineteenth century the engineers **Thomas Telford** and **John McAdam** invented methods of road building that almost doubled the speed at which coaches could travel. The journey from London to Manchester, for example, took four days in 1754, two days in 1784 and 29 hours in 1836. In the 1830s there were about 600 long-distance coach services which travelled to and from London, and a total of 3,300 stage coaches on the roads throughout Britain.

Very few rivers were improved after the 1760s. Instead, a vast amount of money and effort went into the building of canals (source 9). In 1761 the Duke of Bridgewater opened a canal to take coal on the seven-mile journey from his estate to Manchester. As a result he was able to cut the price of the coal from 7d (3p) per ton to 3.5d (1.5p). In the next eleven years schemes were started that eventually linked four major rivers, the Trent, the Mersey, the Severn and the Thames.

In 1760 there were 1,398 miles (2,250 km) of navigable water inland. By 1830 there were 3,875 miles (6,236 km) of which 845 (1,360 km) had been created in the 1790s when Parliament passed 52 Acts allowing new canals to be built.

SOURCE 9

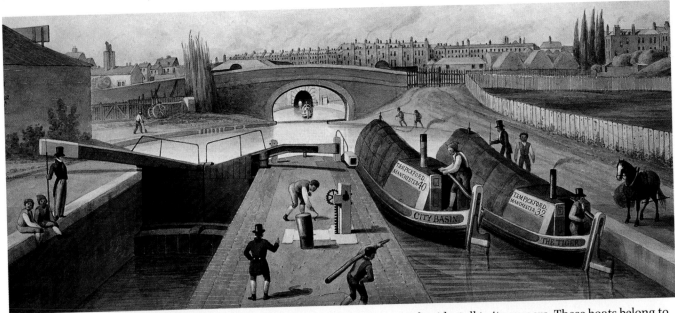

A lock on the Regent's Canal, London, in the 1820s. Companies using a canal paid a toll to its owners. These boats belong to Pickfords. The clerks, in top hats and carrying rods, measured how low the boats floated in the water in order to work out their loads and therefore the tolls payable.

activity

1 What can you learn from sources 8 and 9 about improvements in transport in the late eighteenth and early nineteenth centuries?
2 What were the connections between transport improvements and
a manufacturing
b the rise in population
c demand?

This is how changes in transport helped to make the Industrial Revolution possible:

- Bulky raw materials such as coal and iron could be moved more easily to where they were needed.
- Cheaper transport costs reduced the price of raw materials.
- Food could be moved more easily and cheaply to where it was needed as the population increased.
- Manufactured goods could be taken almost anywhere in Britain. The market for goods therefore became national rather than local.
- Letters, orders for goods, deliveries and business information could all travel more quickly.

Inventions

Cotton was the first industry to go over to mass production by machines in factories. Yet in the early eighteenth century cotton was a new raw material in Britain and very few cotton goods were manufactured compared to woollen and silk goods. Indian cotton goods were cheaper and of higher quality than those from Britain.

British manufacturers, therefore, needed to find ways of making a lot of good quality cloth cheaply. One problem was that it took four or more spinners to supply one weaver with yarn to make cloth. In the 1760s manufacturers offered prizes for inventions that would help spinners to make more yarn.

Source 10 explains some of the inventions that helped the development of the British cotton industry.

SOURCE 10

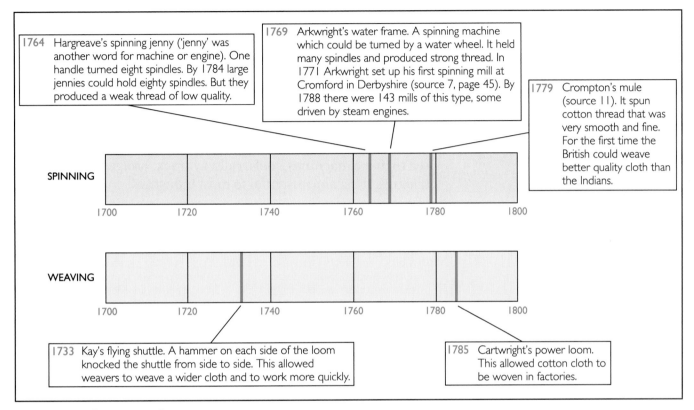

1764 Hargreave's spinning jenny ('jenny' was another word for machine or engine). One handle turned eight spindles. By 1784 large jennies could hold eighty spindles. But they produced a weak thread of low quality.

1769 Arkwright's water frame. A spinning machine which could be turned by a water wheel. It held many spindles and produced strong thread. In 1771 Arkwright set up his first spinning mill at Cromford in Derbyshire (source 7, page 45). By 1788 there were 143 mills of this type, some driven by steam engines.

1779 Crompton's mule (source 11). It spun cotton thread that was very smooth and fine. For the first time the British could weave better quality cloth than the Indians.

SPINNING

1700　1720　1740　1760　1780　1800

WEAVING

1700　1720　1740　1760　1780　1800

1733 Kay's flying shuttle. A hammer on each side of the loom knocked the shuttle from side to side. This allowed weavers to weave a wider cloth and to work more quickly.

1785 Cartwright's power loom. This allowed cotton cloth to be woven in factories.

Inventions in the cotton industry.

SOURCE 11

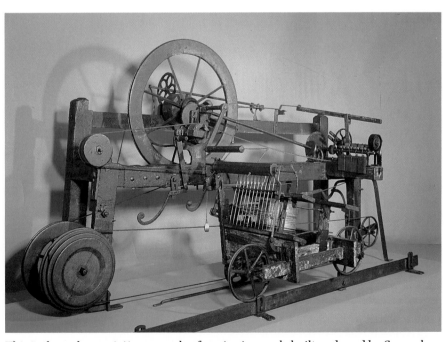

This is the only surviving example of a spinning mule built and used by Samuel Crompton at his Back Kay Street mill in Bolton.

activity

3 Use source 10 and the information in the text.
a Why do you think Kay's invention made things in the cotton industry worse rather than better?
b Why do you think his invention came to be used increasingly after about 1764?

activity

1 What can sources I and II tell you about the various uses of iron?
2 Explain the connection between inventions and
a demand
b mass production.

i **Smelting**   The process of melting an ore in order to get the metal out of it.

Swedish iron was better than British iron and cheaper, too, because wood for making charcoal to burn in **smelting** furnaces was becoming scarce in Britain and therefore expensive. Coal was plentiful and cheap but gave off gases that ruined the molten iron. Source 12 explains how inventions helped the iron industry overcome these problems.

Inventions in the cotton and iron industries helped the Industrial Revolution to happen because they:

- Enabled manufacturers to make cotton goods (i) more quickly, (ii) more cheaply, (iii) from better quality materials. This both supplied demand and helped to increase it.
- Made it possible to make cheaper, good quality iron. This was used to make machines, tools, railway track, bridges and buildings. It became essential to most industries.

SOURCE 12

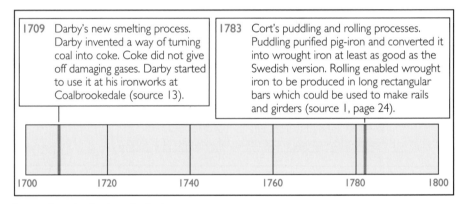

1709   Darby's new smelting process. Darby invented a way of turning coal into coke. Coke did not give off damaging gases. Darby started to use it at his ironworks at Coalbrookedale (source 13).

1783   Cort's puddling and rolling processes. Puddling purified pig-iron and converted it into wrought iron at least as good as the Swedish version. Rolling enabled wrought iron to be produced in long rectangular bars which could be used to make rails and girders (source 1, page 24).

| 1700 | 1720 | 1740 | 1760 | 1780 | 1800 |

Inventions in the iron industry.

SOURCE 13

Coalbrookdale in 1758. Find:
- two blast furnaces in the centre
- a cast-iron cylinder being taken to the River Severn
- coal being turned into coke under piles of wet ashes.

The story of steam

The invention of steam engines to drive machines was one of the most important factors in the development of the Industrial Revolution. Steam engines could do more work than engines worked by the power of water, wind, horses or humans. They drove machines in factories and powered trains and ships. So they made mass production possible and brought about enormous improvements in transport and communications. How did steam engines come to be invented and then to play such an important part in the Industrial Revolution?

Meeting a need

The first steam engines were invented to help tin and coal miners. In the late seventeenth century they sank shafts into the ground rather than digging on the surface. The water that collected was too much for traditional pumps powered by water or horses. Mine owners wanted a pump that could do the job.

SOURCE 14

Newcomen's atmospheric steam engine. It worked on the principle that if you let steam into a cylinder *c* fitted with a piston, and then cool the cylinder with cold water, the steam will condense (turn to water) and create a vacuum. The pressure of the atmosphere will then force the piston down the cylinder. When the vacuum is released the piston can be pulled back up by a counterweight on the other end of a beam *h*. The pump was underground on the ends of rods *i* and *k*. It was worked by the up and down movement of the beam.

activity

1 Why do you think the steam engines they invented were immediately taken up and used in the case of
a Newcomen
b Boulton and Watt?
2 How did the success of Watt's invention depend on
a another inventor
b businessmen?

i Separate condenser

Newcomen engines wasted heat because the cylinder had to be cooled on every stroke to condense the steam (see source 14). This meant the new steam coming in also condensed until it had heated the cylinder back up to boiling water temperature. Watt solved the problem by drawing the steam into a separate chamber where it was condensed, leaving the main cylinder hot.

In 1712, Thomas Newcomen managed to build an 'atmospheric engine' which used steam to work a pump (source 14). By 1750 there were at least 100 Newcomen engines working in Britain and about 550 by 1800. They made a big difference to the tin and coal industries because they enabled miners to work in much deeper mines.

Having the ideas

Inventions depend on the curiosity and cleverness of inventors. One of the biggest steps forward in the development of steam engines happened by chance when James Watt, an instrument maker at Glasgow University, was asked to repair a demonstration model of a Newcomen engine.

Watt noticed the model engine did not work very well even when in good order. He tried to work out why and decided that all Newcomen engines wasted heat. He carried out experiments for two years and then came up with the idea of a **separate condenser**. In 1765 he built a model of a very much improved atmospheric engine.

Money and technology

It is one thing to have a clever idea for an engine; another to build a full-sized version of it. For that, money is needed to pay for labour and materials. Also the right technology has to be available. That is, people have to be able to make the various parts needed for the engine.

James Watt tried to solve both problems by going into partnership with John Roebuck, the founder of the Carron Ironworks near Falkirk. There they built a full-sized engine; but the technology let them down. Roebuck's workers could not make a good enough cylinder. Its diameter varied by as much as 0.95 centimeters which meant the piston could not fit closely and steam escaped.

In 1773 Watt set up a new partnership with Matthew Boulton, owner of the Soho Manufactury, an ironworks outside Birmingham. In 1775 the iron-master John Wilkinson, one of Boulton's friends, solved the technological problem. He invented a machine for boring holes in iron to make gun barrels. This machine could also be used to make iron cylinders to the accuracy Watt needed.

Boulton and Watt engines (source 15) used less than a third of the coal needed by Newcomen engines. So they were much cheaper to run. By 1800 there were about 450 of them working in Britain.

SOURCE 15

A Boulton and Watt engine, 1788. This engine used a system of 'sun and planet' gears to use the up-and-down motion of the beam to turn a wheel. That meant the engine could be used to run machines in mills and factories.

Some inventions were not taken up

To be a success an invention must work *and* it must be used. Some inventions work but are not taken up and used. That was the experience of a Scottish engineer, William Symington, who invented a version of the atmospheric engine capable of driving a boat.

In 1800 Lord Dundas and the directors of the Forth and Clyde Canal Company commissioned Symington to build a steam tug-boat for their canal. After many experiments Symington was ready to try out the tug. On 28 March 1803 the *Charlotte Dundas* (source 16) pulled two boats for nineteen and a half miles (31 kilometres) along the canal near Glasgow against a headwind so strong that no other boats could move at all.

SOURCE 16

The *Charlotte Dundas*. Two boats were built, both named after Lord Dundas's daughter. The first failed. This is the second.

Symington was delighted. He also had an order for eight tugs from the Duke of Bridgewater for the Bridgewater Canal. After this successful trial he could go ahead and build them. Then the news arrived that the Duke was dead and the order cancelled. Meanwhile, to complete his disappointment, the *Charlotte Dundas* failed to enter regular service on the Forth and Clyde.

Symington built no more steamships. Others took up the challenge (source 17).

SOURCE 17

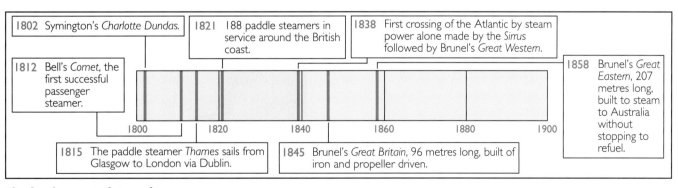

1802 Symington's *Charlotte Dundas*.

1812 Bell's *Comet*, the first successful passenger steamer.

1821 188 paddle steamers in service around the British coast.

1838 First crossing of the Atlantic by steam power alone made by the *Sirius* followed by Brunel's *Great Western*.

1858 Brunel's *Great Eastern*, 207 metres long, built to steam to Australia without stopping to refuel.

1815 The paddle steamer *Thames* sails from Glasgow to London via Dublin.

1845 Brunel's *Great Britain*, 96 metres long, built of iron and propeller driven.

1800   1820   1840   1860   1880   1900

The development of steamships.

Inventors build on each other's work

In 1829 the engineer **Robert Stephenson** built the first steam locomotive, called the *Rocket*, capable of running at speeds of up to 29 m.p.h. (46.7 km p. h.). It was a breakthrough in locomotive design. Once a locomotive could travel so much faster than a horse, building railways to carry passengers became a promising investment.

Robert Stephenson and his father **George** are rightly remembered as the founders of the railway system. But they were building on work begun by Richard Trevithick more than twenty years before.

Between about 1797 and 1802 Trevithick, the son of a tin mine manager in Cornwall, designed a new type of high-pressure steam engine (source 18). It was widely used for pumping and lifting in mines and, after 1812, very powerful versions were used for heavy work such as pumping a town's water supply.

Trevithick had dreams of using his engine in an entirely different way. In 1804 he put it on wheels and used it to drive the first steam locomotive. It pulled ten tonnes of iron bars at 4 m.p.h. (6.8 km p.h.) along a cast-iron tramway from Penydarren ironworks in Merthyr Tydfil to the Glamorganshire canal, about ten miles away.

Trevithick designed a similar locomotive to work at a colliery in Tyneside. This inspired other inventors in the north of England, including George and Robert Stephenson, to invent improved locomotives to pull waggon loads of coal from collieries to the nearest river.

> **i** **George** and **Robert Stephenson** *George Stephenson (1781–1848) started by designing locomotives and tracks for collieries. In 1821 he was chosen to build the Stockton and Darlington railway to carry coal on the twenty-mile journey from the mines to the towns. In 1822 he opened a works in Newcastle with Robert (1803–59), to make locomotives. Between 1827 and 1830 he built the first passenger carrying railway, the Liverpool and Manchester. After that both he and Robert were the engineers for several other railways.*

activity

I People usually remember Robert Stephenson as the inventor of the first successful railway locomotive.
a What claim do you think Richard Trevithick has to that title?
b How do you think he should be remembered?

SOURCE 18

Trevithick's engine, 1802. Unlike Newcomen's and Watt's engines, Trevithick's did not use a vacuum. Instead, steam at very high pressure pushed a piston along a cylinder. A valve then released the steam into the air. The engine was 'direct acting'. That is, it did not use a beam to turn the wheel.

Nasmyth's steam hammer

Nasmyth's steam hammer is an example of an invention that was successful even though it was not needed for its original purpose. In 1839 the engineer **Isambard Kingdom Brunel** was designing a new paddle-steamer, the *Great Britain*. The engine designer found he needed an iron paddle shaft 76.2 centimetres in diameter.

No foundry could make something so big. The designer took the problem to James Nasmyth, a Scot who owned an ironworks and foundry in Manchester, and who had already invented several machines for cutting and shaping metal. Nasmyth's solution was his steam hammer (sources 19 and 20).

SOURCE 19

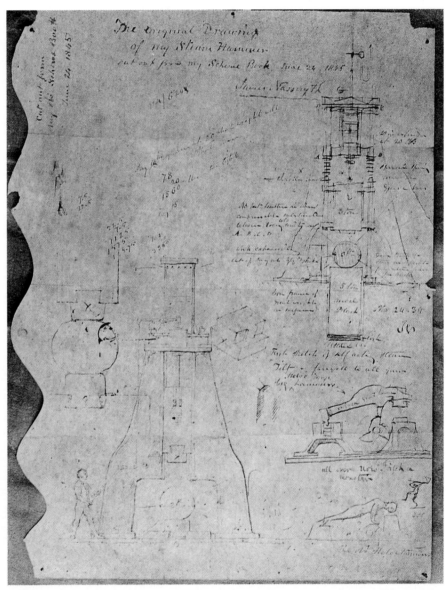

James Nasmyth's original sketch of his steam hammer, 1839. Steam entered the cylinder to raise the piston with the hammer head attached. When the steam was allowed to escape, the hammer fell by its own weight.

activity

2 Look at source 19.
a What can you learn from it about the way in which Nasmyth went about designing his steam hammer?
b What does it tell you about Nasmyth's various skills?

At this point, Brunel decided to use a propeller instead of paddles to drive the *Great Britain*. Although the hammer was no longer needed for its original purpose, it still met a need. It was an important invention because for the first time iron workers could make very large engine parts. It was also very versatile. According to a description in the catalogue of the Great Exhibition, the hammer could be adjusted so finely that 'it could descend with power only sufficient to break an egg shell'.

SOURCE 20

James Nasmyth's steam hammer, painted by Nasmyth himself in about 1842.

assignments

1 Use the sources and information on pages 12–14 and 22 in Part 2 and pages 30–32 and 37 in Part 3.
a Describe the changes that took place in transport between 1750 and 1850.
b What do you think stayed the same?

2 Work in pairs and use the sources and information on pages 26–34. Take each of the following factors:

- Population
- Trade
- Agriculture
- Transport
- Inventions

a (i) List all the contributions you think each factor made to the Industrial Revolution. (ii) Decide whether you think each contribution was a long-term or a short-term cause. (iii) Discuss your decisions with other pairs.
b Make a chart to show the links between each of the factors.
c In a group, discuss how important you think each factor was in helping to cause the Industrial Revolution.
d Why do you think historians find it difficult to explain exactly what triggered off the Industrial Revolution?

3 Work in pairs. Imagine a museum wishes to put up a wall display, using words, pictures and diagrams, to show junior school children some of the causes and consequences of the development of steam power. You have been commissioned to make this. Use the sources and information on pages 12–14, and 16–22 in Part 2, on pages 35–40 in Part 3, and books from libraries to help you.

4 Use the sources and information about steam power on pages 35–40.
a How do they show that inventors often needed the help of (i) people with money, (ii) people with experience in business or manufacturing, (iii) other inventors?
b Some inventions are taken up and used immediately. Some are not. Choose (i) an invention to do with steam power that was taken up immediately, (ii) one that was not, and in each case explain why you think this was.

5 Each of the following factors helped to cause the increase in the use of steam power:

- the needs of people working in various industries
- inventors
- people willing to give money so that inventors could try out their ideas
- improved technology.

Say:
a what you think each factor contributed
b how you rank the four factors in order of importance, giving your reasons
c in what ways you think the four factors are connected.

4
A Golden Age?

The Industrial Revolution brought great changes to Britain, in particular the move towards mass production in factories and the growth of industrial cities. In Part 2 you looked at some of these changes and the impact they had on people's lives. Part 4 is about whether the changes were for better or for worse. In 'A golden age?' you can make up your mind about two conflicting interpretations of the domestic system of the eighteenth century. In 'Progress for whom?' you can decide who benefited most from the great changes.

A golden age?

Different interpretations

Some people in the nineteenth century disliked the factory system. They saw the domestic system of the eighteenth century as a golden age when things were made by families living happily in cottages in the countryside. Since then many historians have taken the same view.

Other historians argue that the domestic system had as many problems as advantages for the people working in it. They say the benefits the factory system brought to workers outweighed the hardships.

Who is right? You will have to make up your mind about two things:

- How good was life in the eighteenth-century domestic system of manufacturing?
- Was life in the nineteenth-century factory system much worse or a bit better?

The domestic system

The craftspeople who worked at home in the domestic system worked with their families and shared the tasks. A nineteenth-century doctor, Peter Gaskell, pictured them in a thatched cottage.

SOURCE 1

A reconstruction of the inside of a weaver's cottage about 1800, at the York Castle Museum.

He said it brought them 'happy memories and home delights'. The reality was probably less cosy (source 1). This is how Gaskell described the years before 1760:

SOURCE 2

These were, undoubtedly, the golden times of manufactures . . . By all the processes being carried on under a man's own roof, he retained his . . . respectability . . . whilst he generally earned wages which were sufficient not only to live comfortably upon, but which enabled him to rent a few acres of land.

Peter Gaskell, writing in the early nineteenth century

activity

1a Look at source 2 (above). Why does Peter Gaskell think that the years before 1760 were 'the golden times of manufactures'?
b Do (i) source 1, (ii) source 5, (iii) source 6 suggest Gaskell's statement might be right or wrong? Give your reasons.

Workers in the domestic system enjoyed the freedom to organise their own time and to work when they pleased. They were paid 'piece rates', that is money for each item produced rather than for the time it took to make it. Many of them did not work on Monday, calling it 'Saint Monday' (source 3) because they treated it as a holiday. Then they worked harder and faster on each of the following days so that they could finish the week's job on time.

SOURCE 3

Saint Monday. How many different craftspeople are shown? What are they doing with their time off?

Some of those who could afford it chose to work fewer hours so as to have more free time. According to William Hutton, who had been a framework knitter in the 1730s and 1740s:

SOURCE 4

If a man can support his family with three days labour, he will not work six.

William Hutton, *A History of Birmingham*, 1781

Samuel Bamford worked in the domestic system towards the end of the eighteenth century. He remembered how the putter-out often took a glass of ale in the pub with the weavers when they came to deliver finished cloth and collect more material:

SOURCE 5

The business betwixt workman and putter-out was generally done in an amicable [friendly], reasonable way. No ... fault-finding, no bullying, no arbitrary abatement [stopping of wages], which have been too common since, were practised.

Samuel Bamford, *Early Days*, 1849

But William Hutton, who left weaving to set up as a bookseller, remembered harder times. He looked back sadly on the lives of his grandfather, father and uncle, all of whom worked in the cloth-making trade:

Their weekly earnings being small, and consumed as soon as earned, nothing has remained for sickness, age or accident . . . Where should I have been now if I had continued a stockinger [weaver]? I must have been in the workhouse. They all go there when they cannot see to work.

William Hutton, *Life of William Hutton*, written in the late eighteenth century

The factory system

activity

1 Use source 7 and the information in the text. What differences did factories make to people's
a working
b family lives?

For those who went to work in factories for the first time in the late eighteenth and early nineteenth centuries, life changed completely. Some came from the domestic system, some from farming where they were used to working in the hours of daylight and to the rhythm of the seasons.

Factory owners did not recognise the hours of daylight. Machines could run round the clock (source 7). They wanted their workers to work regular hours and not to take time off when they pleased. If workers were late, or were caught slacking, they were fined. Bells told them when to start work and when to stop.

SOURCE 7

Richard Arkwright's cotton mill, Cromford, painted by Joseph Wright of Derby, about 1789. The mill took its power from the River Derwent. One water-wheel drove hundreds of spindles for spinning the cotton. It was lit by candles at night.

Many families relied on every member of the family earning a wage. Women and children went off to the factories each day as well as men. But they did not necessarily work together on the same shift, nor even in the same factory.

In the nineteenth century some people contrasted the freedom of domestic workers with the fate of factory workers who were held captive by the demands of machines:

SOURCE 8

Whilst the engine runs the people must work – men , women and children are yoked together with iron and steam. The animal machine . . . is chained fast to the iron machine, which knows no suffering and no weariness.

James Kay-Shuttleworth, *The Moral and Physical Condition of the Working Classes Employed in the Cotton Manufacture in Manchester, written in the mid-nineteenth century*

They said that people were no longer important. The masters who owned the factories thought only of profit:

SOURCE 9

The work people are less thought of than the machinery . . . Care is seldom taken that the animal machine sustain as little injury as possible, and that it will bear the work imposed.

C. Turner Thackrah, *The Effects of Arts, Trades and Professions . . . on Health and Longevity*, 1832

Others sang the praises of machines because they saved people from hard, dreary work:

SOURCE 11

In my recent tour . . . through the manufacturing districts, I have seen tens of thousands of old, young and middle-aged of both sexes . . . earning abundant food . . . without perspiring at a single pore.

Andrew Ure, *Philosophy of Manufactures*, 1835

Many thought the factory system was evil because it encouraged the employment of young children in dangerous and unpleasant conditions (source 10). Robert Owen, himself a factory owner, thought it wrong that:

SOURCE 12

In the manufacturing districts it is common for parents to send their children of both sexes at seven or eight years of age . . . at six o'clock in the morning, sometimes . . . . in the dark, and occasionally amidst frost and snow, to enter the manufactories, which are often heated to a high temperature.

Robert Owen, *Observations on the Effect of the Manufacturing System*, 1815

activity

Work in pairs.
1 Look at source 10.
a What does it tell you about working conditions in factories?
b How reliable do you think it is as evidence? Give your reasons.

SOURCE 10

An illustration from *The Life and Adventures of Michael Armstrong, Factory Boy*, written in 1840 by Francis Trollope, who supported the campaign against children's work.

activity

2 Peter Gaskell made the statement that the eighteenth century saw 'the golden times of manufactures'. Look at sources 7–14. Which sources do you think provide arguments that could be used to
a support Gaskell's statement
b attack it?
3 Use all the sources and information in Part 4 so far to make a list of arguments
a for Gaskell's opinion
b against it.

Factory workers faced long hours of work, often from six o'clock in the morning to noon, with an hour for lunch and then on again until eight o'clock at night. Peter Gaskell thought this was bad, but for him the 'great curse' of the factory system was:

SOURCE 13

In the breaking up of all home and social affections: the father, the mother and the child are alike all occupied and never meet under the common roof except in the evenings.

Peter Gaskell, *Prospects of Industry*, 1835

Richard Guest approved of the factory system because it brought people together and sharpened their minds. He contrasted dull, unthinking domestic workers sitting 'vacant and inactive in each others' houses' with factory workers who held intelligent conversations:

SOURCE 14

The questions of Peace and War, which interested them importantly, inasmuch as they might produce a rise or fall of wages, became highly interesting, and this brought them into the vast field of politics.

Richard Guest, 1823

Progress for whom?

The Industrial Revolution brought what the writer Samuel Smiles called 'a harvest of wealth and prosperity' to many people. The question is, did everybody's life improve or did some lose out while others gained? It was in the nineteenth century that people first began to talk of British society being divided into three main groups: the upper, middle and working classes. How did the Industrial Revolution affect people in each of these groups?

The upper and middle classes

Among the first people to gain from the industrial revolution were wealthy lords and their families. In the 1780s they bought the latest products in cotton materials, pottery and iron. At the same time new factory masters and many merchants made their fortunes and could afford to build and furnish fine houses.

Smaller business people, professional people and shopkeepers grew wealthier in the early nineteenth century. They also benefited from the lower prices of manufactured goods. The writer G. R. Porter pointed out that prosperous shopkeepers in London around 1800 had no carpets in their sitting rooms, whereas in 1851:

SOURCE 15

In the same houses we now see, not carpets merely, but many articles of furniture which were formerly in use only among the nobility and gentry: the walls are now covered with paintings or engravings . . .

G. R. Porter, *The Progress of the Nation,* 1851

Upper-class and middle-class families were the first to use the new roads and railways, and to take holidays at the seaside. They lived in the cleaner and healthier suburbs of towns. They could afford to live in comfort (source 16) with servants to look after them.

SOURCE 16

The parlour of a middle-class home in the 1870s.

The working classes

Skilled workers

Among the working class, skilled workers gained the most from the Industrial Revolution. Some, such as woolcombers and calico-printers, were put out of work by the new machines; but at the same time new skilled trades came into demand. Iron puddlers, engine drivers, engineers and fitters, and fine cotton spinners all joined the ranks of skilled workers who were paid one and a half to two times as much as the average worker in their trade. It was they who:

SOURCE 17

Ate meat, vegetables, fruit and dairy produce, lived in the best and newest cottages and filled them with furniture and knick-knacks, bought books and newspapers . . .

H. Perkin, *The Origins of Modern English Society 1780–1880*, 1967

Unskilled workers

Male factory workers were paid up to three times more than agricultural workers in the north of England (who were better paid than those in the south); but they could be thrown out of work whenever there was a fall in demand for the goods they made (source 18, page 50). Also, they had to work very long hours, often in very bad conditions.

For the first half of the nineteenth century at least, they lived in very bad conditions, too (see Part 2, pages 17–18). Male miners, ironworkers and railway workers also earned more than agricultural workers. Women and children always earned far less than men working in the same occupation.

The handloom weavers

The story of the handloom weavers shows how the Industrial Revolution could first help a group of workers and then harm them. From the 1770s to the 1790s weavers working at home earned very high wages. There was a great demand for cotton cloth and the new spinning machines (see page 33) provided plenty of yarn.

Seeing the high earnings to be made, many people set up as weavers. By about 1800 the trade was becoming overcrowded. Then came the introduction of steam-powered weaving machines in factories. Handloom weavers were hardly needed.

The weekly earnings of Bolton weavers fell from 25s (£1.25) in 1800 to 5s (25p) or less in the 1830s. There were 250,000 weavers in 1830 and only 23,000 in 1856. Thousands were put out of work by the Industrial Revolution and joined the ranks of the unskilled poor, desperately trying to make a living in the cities.

activity

1 What do the sources and information on pages 47–49 suggest about the ways in which the Industrial Revolution improved the lives of
a the middles classes
b skilled workers?
2 Do you think the Industrial Revolution would have been described as 'progress' by
a the middle classes
b skilled workers?
Give your reasons.

activity

3 Do you think a handloom weaver might have described the Industrial Revolution as 'progress' in
a 1790
b 1830?
Give your reasons.

SOURCE 18

Factory closed – a starving workman and his family. An engraving from *The British Workman*, December 1862.

Workers in the countryside

As you have seen in Part 2, mass production in factories eventually destroyed many jobs in the countryside (page 20). Even so, the Industrial Revolution also brought benefits. For instance, when factories appeared in the north of England in the late eighteenth and early nineteenth centuries, the wages of agricultural workers in the region went up. Farmers had to pay their labourers more in order to stop them leaving for better-paid factory work.

SOURCE 19

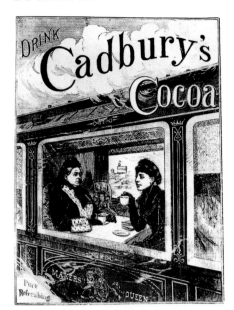

A newspaper advertisement for Cadbury's Cocoa, showing Queen Victoria drinking cocoa in a train.

Similarly the construction of a railway network in Wales caused farm wages to rise by between 33 and 50 per cent. The railway meant workers could more easily move to better-paid work in the mines and ironworks of Monmouth and Glamorgan. So, again, farmers had to raise wages to keep them.

Better food

The Industrial Revolution also meant that people's diets slowly improved. By 1900 people of all classes, living in both town and countryside, were able to buy a much wider variety of food than people living in 1750.

The railways cut down the time it took to transport goods from one place to another. Until they were built, perishable food such as fish, which stayed fresh for a short time and then went off very quickly, could be eaten only by people living close to seaports or freshwater sources. In the 1860s trains began to carry fish all over the country from ports such as Grimsby and Hull.

Trains also carried meat, milk and other produce from the country to the town. They carried milk to London from as far away as Derbyshire and Dorset, and milk from Leicestershire to Leeds and Newcastle.

They also carried goods with brand names, such as Pears Soap and Cadbury's Cocoa, from the factories to shops and customers all over the country (source 19).

Towards the end of the century new factory processes meant people could buy tinned foods. These were popular in the country as well as the town:

SOURCE 20

At the village shops there is an increased demand for tinned meats of all kinds.

Royal Commission on Labour, 1893–94

---

activity

1 Look at source 19.
a Why do you think advertisers liked to use the Queen in their posters?
b Cadbury's cocoa was made in Birmingham. (i) Why was it easier to sell it throughout the country after the coming of the railways? (ii) Why might cocoa made by a small local firm have been more expensive than Cadbury's?
2 Look at source 20. Why do you think tinned meats might have been so popular?

assignments

1 Some people have seen the days of the domestic system as a golden age for manufacturing workers compared to the days of the factory system.
a Would you agree if you used (i) only sources 3 and 6; (ii) only sources 2 and 5?
b Use all the sources and information on 'A golden age?', pages 42–47 and, in Part 2, pages 15–23. Organise a class discussion about the strengths and weaknesses of this interpretation.

2a Peter Gaskell believed the conditions in factories in his own times were very bad. How might that have influenced his interpretation of eighteenth-century domestic industry?
b The historian V. H. H. Green thought some modern historians shared Peter Gaskell's feelings:

SOURCE 21

Historians . . . in their zeal [enthusiasm] to disclose [expose] the evil results of the factory system, have often painted the industrial worker under the domestic system in rosy colours.

V. H. H. Green, *The Hanoverians*, 1948

Use the sources and information on pages 42–47 to write two short comparisons of life in the domestic and factory systems, as you think they might be written (i) by an historian who believes the factory system was full of evils; (ii) by an historian who is trying to give the most accurate possible picture.

3 Use the sources and information on pages 47–51.
a (i) Describe how the changes brought about by the Industrial Revolution caused the living standards of some people to improve and of others to get worse. (ii) Explain what this tells you about the relationship between change and progress.
b (i) Explain why the same group of people, for example the handloom weavers, could find their living standards going up at one time and down at another. (ii) What does this suggest to you about patterns of change?

4 Use the sources and information in Parts 2 and 3. Make a chart to show the various ways in which the Industrial Revolution affected either (i) different parts of Britain, or (ii) different social groups.

5 Look at the sources and information on pages 47–51 and, in Part 2, pages 17–23.
a (i) Which people living and working in the countryside might have described the changes caused by the Industrial Revolution as 'progress'? (ii) Which might not? Give your reasons.
b How do they suggest that the effects of the Industrial Revolution were felt by different groups of people at different times?

5

Trade and Empire

Trade with other countries was always important to the British people (source 1). Between 1750 and 1900 they became increasingly dependent upon it. At the same time big changes took place in the type of goods they bought and sold, and the markets around the world in which they bought and sold them.

In 1750 the British also ruled many of the territories with which they traded. Many of these colonies started in the late sixteenth and seventeenth centuries as settlements of British merchants, or of people looking for a new life abroad. After 1750 the territories ruled by Britain grew until they included about a quarter of the world's land and a fifth of its population.

The first section of Part 5 is about the growth and development of Britain's empire and trade. In the second section you will be able to investigate some of the effects of the British Empire on the way of life and attitudes of the British people.

SOURCE 1

A ship flying the flag of the East India Company, painted in about 1720. Ships like this carried most of Britain's long-distance trade until the nineteenth century. During the nineteenth century, large iron, then steel, sailing ships replaced them. These were in turn gradually replaced by steam ships.

The British Empire

Source 2 shows how the British Empire expanded in the eighteenth and nineteenth centuries. It grew in three main ways. The first was through trade. Merchants might set up a trading post in a country and then decide the best way to protect their trade was to take over as rulers. This happened in India, where the East India Company took over Indian lands in the eighteenth century.

The second way was through war and conquest. In the late eighteenth and early nineteenth centuries many of the wars were against other European countries, such as France, with which Britain was competing for colonies. Sometimes the wars were against the rulers of a state which appeared to threaten the British in an existing colony.

The third way was through exploration. Explorers, like Captain Cook in the Pacific in the late eighteenth century (see page 55) and David Livingstone in Africa in the mid-nineteenth (see pages 67–69), explored lands previously unknown to Europeans. Later they were followed by merchants or settlers or both.

SOURCE 2a

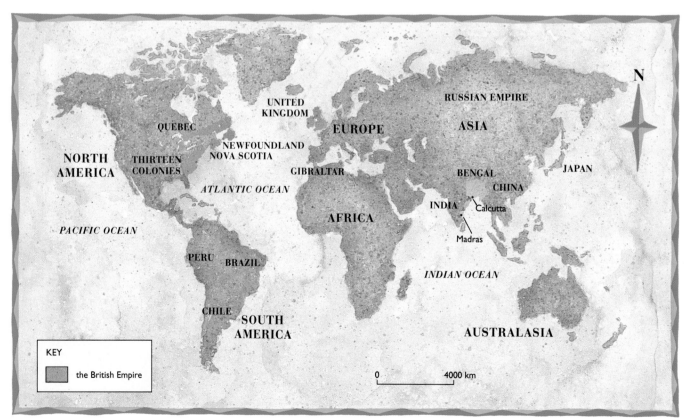

The Empire in 1765. In a series of successful wars against France, ending in 1763, Britain added French-held territories in Canada and India to those it already held in North America and the Caribbean (see source 4, page 57). In India the new territories were governed by the East India Company, which also took over as the formal ruler of Bengal in 1765.

SOURCE 2b

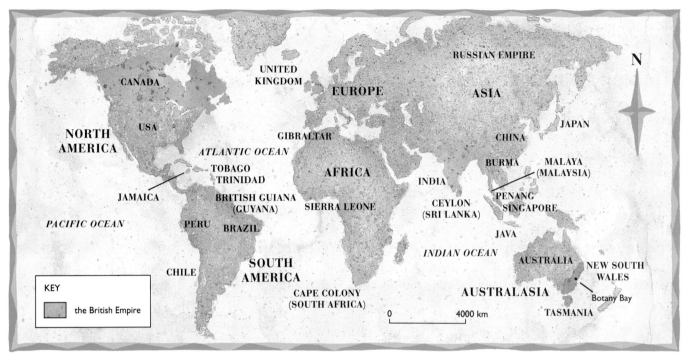

The Empire in 1830. In 1776 the Thirteen Colonies broke away to form the United States of America. During wars with France (1793–1815) Britain took over French, Spanish and Dutch-held lands in the Caribbean, and Dutch-held territories in Ceylon (now Sri Lanka) and the Cape Colony (now South Africa). The East India Company expanded its control in India, Burma and Malaya (now Malaysia). In 1770 Captain Cook landed at Botany Bay in Australia and claimed it for Britain. From 1788 convicts were transported there. Many settled after their release. Transportation ended in 1849.

SOURCE 2c

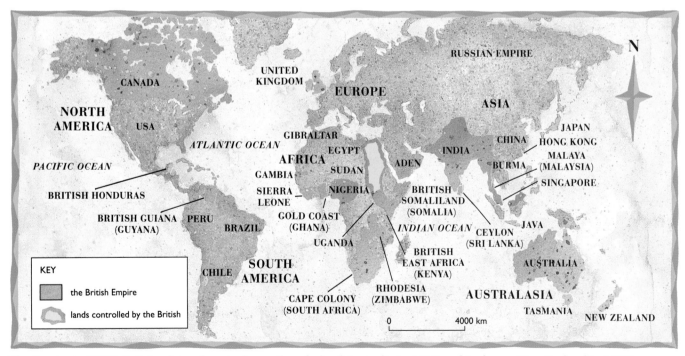

The Empire in 1900. Britain claimed control over the whole of Australia in 1829 and took over New Zealand in 1840. Britain also extended its control of territories in India, Burma, Malaya and the Pacific Ocean. In 1858 the East India Company was dissolved and the Government ruled India directly. After about 1870 Britain took control over vast territories in Africa, where France and Germany were also competing to build large empires.

Trade

Changing patterns

Between 1750 and 1900 trade became increasingly important to Britain. As a result of the Industrial Revolution, manufacturers had goods to sell that no other country made, so they could sell to markets worldwide. At the same time, they needed to import raw materials to make more products. Britain had some supplies of metal ores, such as iron and tin, but not nearly enough. They also needed cotton and wool for making textiles.

On top of that, the British people needed food. The population had grown too large to be fed by British farmers alone. In the nineteenth century Britain relied on raw materials and food from all over the world (source 3).

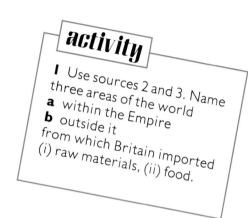

activity

1 Use sources 2 and 3. Name three areas of the world
a within the Empire
b outside it
from which Britain imported (i) raw materials, (ii) food.

SOURCE 3

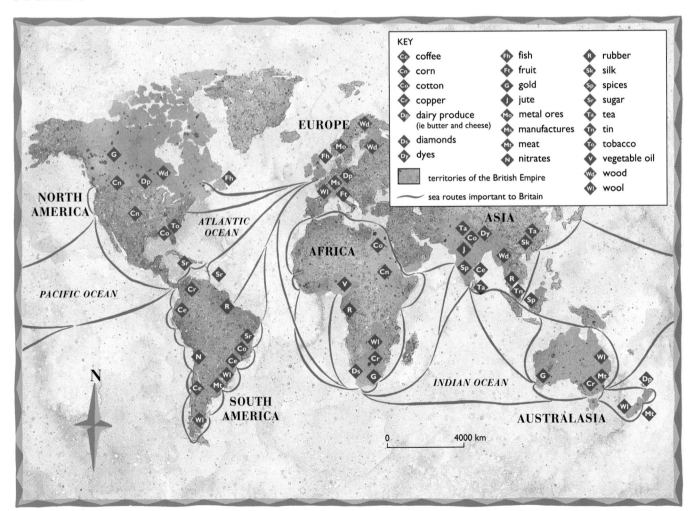

Britain's imports in the nineteenth century. The symbols show the goods Britain imported and the parts of the world from which they came.

The pattern of the goods Britain exported in exchange for her imports gradually changed (source 4). At the start of the nineteenth century textiles were by far the biggest export. By 1900, Britain was exporting larger amounts of other goods as other industries grew in importance.

SOURCE 4

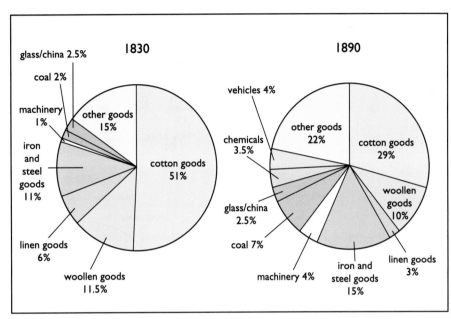

The changing pattern of British exports. The charts show the percentage amounts contributed by different types of goods to the total of exports in 1830 and 1890.

The pattern of Britain's trade with different regions of the world also changed (source 5). The eighteenth-century trading network, which had centred on the slave trade to the West Indies (Part 3, source 3), was replaced by a network based on the worldwide export of manufactured goods and the import of raw materials and food. Trade with the West Indies declined, while trade with North and South America, Australia and New Zealand gradually increased. Europe, however, remained Britain's most important trading partner throughout.

Source 5 reveals another interesting point. Look at the figures for the total values of imports and exports. Britain paid out more money on imports than it received for exports. It had what is called a 'trade deficit'. That is, the British bought more goods from other countries than they sold to them.

If a person spends more than he earns, he gets into debt and eventually ends up bankrupt. The same applies to countries. So why did it not happen to Britain? The answer is, the British made money from things other than manufactured goods, particularly from shipping, banking and insurance services, and investing money abroad. This meant that the 'balance of payments' (the overall account showing how much was spent and how much was earned abroad) showed a profit.

activity

2 Use source 4 and the information in the text.
a Make a list of the British exports which (i) grew, (ii) declined between 1830 and 1890.
b Which (i) grew, (ii) declined the most?
3 Look at source 5.
a From which areas of the world did Britain's imports (i) increase, (ii) decrease between 1794–96 and 1900?
b To which areas did Britain's exports (i) increase, (ii) decrease?

SOURCE 5

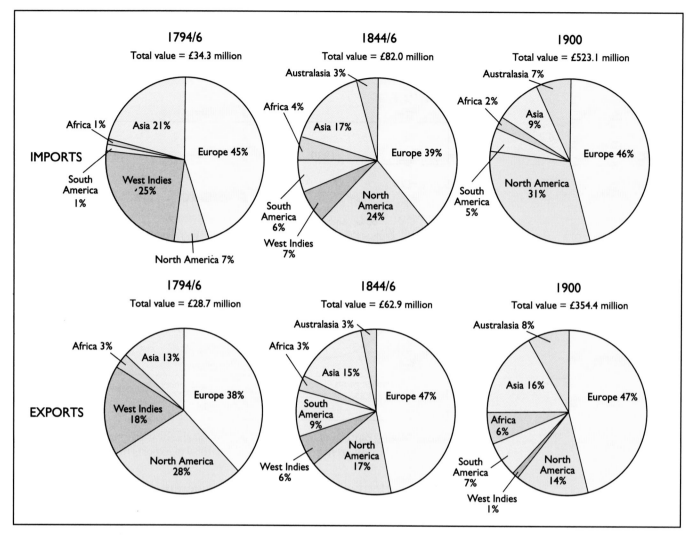

The value of Britain's trade with different regions of the world. The chart shows the percentage of the total value of imports and exports taken up by each region.

The 'informal empire'

By the mid-nineteenth century Britain was in a very powerful position in the world because it was the first country to have an industrial revolution. People in other countries wanted to buy British manufactured goods because they were cheap and often the only ones available. They wanted to pay for British skills, such as railway engineering. They also wanted to borrow British money to help them build roads and railways and buy machinery.

SOURCE 6

A railway bridge over a gorge in São Paolo, Brazil, designed and built by British engineers in the nineteenth century. In Argentina, British engineers built the railways and ran the trains. In return the Argentinian government guaranteed them a minimum profit of 7 per cent.

> **i** **Consul**   A government official appointed to live in a foreign town to look after British subjects and trading rights there.

SOURCE 8

Country	Approximate date of Industrial Revolution
Britain	1780
Belgium	1830
France	1830
Germany	1850
USA	1865
Japan	1890

Industrial revolutions, 1780–1900. The table shows the approximate starting date of each country's industrial revolution.

All this made Britain just as powerful in some countries which were not part of the Empire as it was in the ones that were. Many South American countries, for example, formed part of this 'informal empire' (source 6). Writing about the *gaucho*, the South American cowboy, the British **consul** in Buenos Aires said:

SOURCE 7

> *If his wife had a gown, ten to one it was made in Manchester; the camp kettle in which he cooks his food, the earthenware he eats from, his poncho, spurs, bit, all are imported from England.*

> Quoted in L. Bethell, *Empire in El Dorado, 1972*

Was Britain 'the workshop of the world'?

Britain was not the only country to have an industrial revolution (source 8). By the 1870s Germany and the USA rivalled Britain in their output of raw materials and manufacturered goods. Whereas in 1850 Britain produced most of the world's output of coal, iron, steel and cotton cloth, in 1890 it produced a much smaller percentage of it (source 9).

SOURCE 9

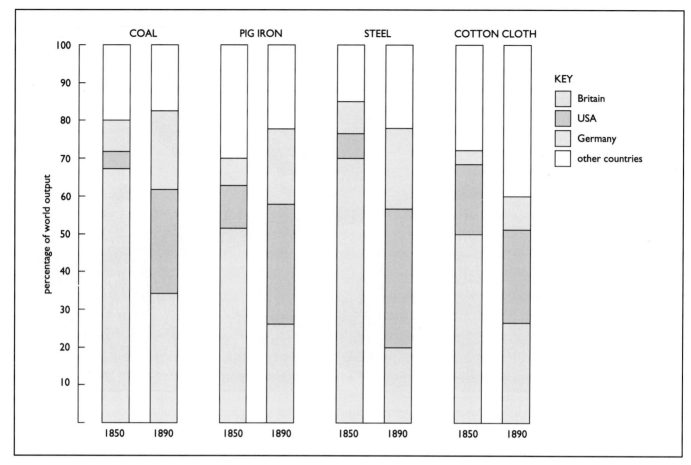

Britain in world industry in the nineteenth century. The graphs show each country's percentage contribution to the world's output of coal, pig iron, steel and cotton cloth in 1850 and 1890.

As other countries industrialised, they wanted British products less. Britain's trade with them declined and Britain began to rely increasingly on exporting to less-developed countries, mainly within the Empire. Although by 1900 Britain was only one among several industrialised nations, it managed to keep its lead in providing the world with capital as well as with shipping, banking, and insurance services.

activity

1a What do sources 6 and 7 tell you about the things South America needed from Britain?
b Did Britain need anything from South America (sources 3 and 5)?
2 Look at sources 8 and 9. In the mid-nineteenth century some people called Britain 'the workshop of the world'.
a What do you think they meant?
b Do you think they were right (i) in 1850, (ii) at the end of the nineteenth century?

The effects of Empire

The Empire affected the British people in various ways. To many it offered the chance of a new way of life abroad. To those who stayed in Britain the Empire remained a rather vague idea until the late nineteenth century, when they became much more aware of it.

Opportunities abroad

The Empire offered the British people the chance to start a new life in a different country. In Canada, Australia and New Zealand, in particular, there appeared to be plenty of land waiting to be settled and, with it, the opportunity for a family to make a fresh start. Millions of people decided to take their chance and go. They faced a long and often unpleasant sea voyage and they left behind the people and places they knew for those they did not. What made them do it?

The main reason was that the huge rise in the population of Britain and Ireland (Part 2, source 1) meant that in many places there were not enough jobs, houses and food to go round. In the past this might have meant that people would have starved to death. In the nineteenth century, however, there was an escape route: emigration.

The problem was particularly severe in Ireland where most people lived off the land. About three million Irish people lived in dreadful poverty and survived by eating potatoes. Few landlords had introduced the agricultural improvements seen in England, so the land produced less food than it could. The crop that did best in the wet undrained soil was the potato. But in 1845 and 1846 the potato crop failed. During the 'Potato Famine' which followed, one million people died of starvation. Between 1845 and 1851 another million left Ireland.

Many people emigrated from Scotland, too, about 640,000 between 1830 and 1880 (source 10). Many of them were poor families from the Highlands where new landlords were throwing out households who had lived there for generations in order to make way for profitable sheep farming. Unlike the old clan chiefs, whom they bought out, the new landlords had no interest in looking after the clanspeople.

Not all Scottish emigrants were trying to escape poverty and starvation. Some were farming families from various parts of the country who simply wanted the chance to own their own land and increase their wealth.

SOURCE 10

'Lochaber No More', painted by J. Wilson Nicol in 1863. Most Scots went to the USA, or to Canada where many had settled in the eighteenth century.

i Missionaries Members of a 'mission', an organisation which tries to convert people to the Christian faith. Many missionary societies in the nineteenth century sent missionaries to try to convert people living in the Empire.

Many English emigrants came from the farming regions of the south where wages were low and there were few jobs. Property owners who had to pay Poor Rates to support the unemployed were usually helpful. Sometimes landlords paid for the sea-passages of their labourers and in some parishes Emigration Committees were set up to help people to go abroad.

By far the largest number of emigrants from the British Isles went to the United States of America. Within the Empire they went mainly to Canada, Australia, New Zealand and the Cape Colony (now South Africa). Many Irish people settled in England.

In 1832 a labourer from Sussex, George Sullington, emigrated with his wife to Canada. He wrote back to his parents:

SOURCE 11

I like the country here very much, but my wife don't seem quite so well contented yet. I got work the first day I was here, and have had plenty of work ever since . . . Farmers and labourers all sit at one table here. I don't wish to persuade anyone to come over, for they must expect to see a good many hardships; but I know that a poor man can do a great deal better here than he can at home: he is sure to get plenty of work if he is steady, and can live cheaper . . . Dear Father and Mother, we left you almost broken hearted, but you must be satisfied that we have bettered our condition by coming here . . .

Revd T. Sockett (ed.), *Letters from Sussex Emigrants*, 1832

Those who emigrated to colonies such as Canada, Australia and New Zealand were mainly working-class people: labourers, craftspeople, factory workers and domestic servants. The Empire also offered opportunities to middle-class emigrants. The colonies in Africa and Asia, in particular, provided many professional people with careers as administrators, doctors, engineers, soldiers and **missionaries**.

Food and goods

For most British people the most obvious impact of the Empire on their daily lives was the availability of foods and other goods (source 3, page 56). Tobacco, sugar and tea from the colonies, all luxuries in 1700, had become cheap enough to be essentials for many families in 1800.

In the 1880s Britain was also able to import large quantities of cheap frozen meat and dairy produce from countries such as Canada, Australia and New Zealand. This was made possible by the invention of refrigeration and the development of big ocean-going steamers.

Corn had been imported from the USA since the 1870s. The availability of all this food from abroad drove down the price of food in Britain in the later nineteenth century. This created improvement in the standard of living, even for some of the poorest people.

The big tea, cocoa, soap and cigarette firms, whose products came from various parts of the Empire, used several methods to get this message across to the British public. For example, they often used pictures of the Empire in their advertising (source 12). The two big soap firms, Pears and Lever Brothers, also started to produce books for children which were published each year and called 'Annuals'.

Annuals contained information as well as stories. Lever Brothers' *Sunlight Annual*, named after their headquarters on Merseyside, Port Sunlight, and their 'Sunlight Soap', was first published in 1894. The 1899 edition contained a section called 'The States of the World' which included 23 pages on the British Empire and nine on the rest of the world. There were diagrams to show the increase in the produce sent from countries of the Empire to Britain during the 1890s and a map showing Port Sunlight's position as an importer of products from the Empire and an exporter of goods worldwide.

Towards the end of the nineteenth century school history and geography books told children what each country of the Empire produced and explained the importance of this to the British people.

SOURCE 12

An advertisement for Lipton's tea, late nineteenth century.

activity

1 Look at source 13.
a What connections does source 13 suggest between the Empire, the people of Britain, steamships and warships?
b What do you think pupils in 1911 learnt about the Empire when they read this poem?

i Rudyard Kipling
Rudyard Kipling (1865–1936) was an English writer, born in India. He was a strong supporter of the Empire. Many of his stories and poems were set in India, including a novel, Kim, and some of his books for children such as The Jungle Book and Just So Stories.

Here are some stanzas of a poem called 'Big Steamers' which **Rudyard Kipling** wrote for a school history book in 1911:

SOURCE 13

'Oh, where are you going to, all you Big Steamers,
With England's own coal, up and down the salt seas?'
'We are going to fetch you your bread and your butter,
Your beef, port, and mutton, eggs, apples and cheese.'

'And where will you fetch it from, all you Big Steamers,
And where shall I write to you when you are away?'
'We fetch it from Melbourne, Quebec, and Vancouver,
Address us at Hobart, Hong-Kong and Bombay.'

. . .

'Then what can I do for you, all you Big Steamers,
Oh, what can I do for your comfort and good?'
'Send out your big warships to watch your big waters,
That no one may stop us from bringing you food.

For the bread that you eat and the biscuits you nibble,
The sweets that you suck and the joints that you carve,
They are brought to you daily by all us Big Steamers,
And if anyone hinders our coming you'll starve!'

Rudyard Kipling, 'Big Steamers', 1911

Patriotism

Between the middle of the eighteenth and the middle of the nineteenth centuries, most British people were not much aware of the Empire. In the second half of the nineteenth century they became more conscious of its existence, as newspapers carried stories of the exploits of British explorers and missionaries like David Livingstone (see Part 6, pages 67–68)

Then, in the 1880s and 1890s, when Britain was competing with other European countries to take over territories in Africa, many people became very enthusiastic about the Empire and proud to be British because of it. Music hall songs became very patriotic and celebrated military victories and heroes of the Empire. They were then often issued as sheet music, with a colour picture on the cover, to be played on the **piano** and sung at home (source 14).

Pride in the army and navy, and interest in the Empire, were also stimulated by cigarette cards. These were issued by companies making products such as tea and sweets as well as by tobacco companies. The main subjects were sports, music hall performers, the armed forces, transport and the Empire. The Empire sets included colonial regiments, flags of the countries of the Empire,

i Piano Music at home became a popular pastime for the middle classes in particular. Between 1870 and 1910 the production and sales of pianos increased five times, eventually reaching about 100,000 a year.

SOURCE 14

'Sons of the Sea'. This popular music hall song was written in 1896 by Felix McGlennon, an Irish-born emigrant to the USA.

SOURCE 15

Postcards of an Indian Table Servant and a 'Dhobi' (washerman). Cards like these first appeared in 1899. Other sets included British and colonial army regiments, guns, naval ships, new buildings in the Empire and colonial products.

scenes, peoples and products of the Empire, and builders of the Empire.

Sets of postcards were issued too (source 15). Companies which relied on the Empire for their products also helped to stir up a feeling of pride in it. Tea, biscuit and tobacco companies often decorated the tins and boxes they used to package their products with pictures of the royal family, famous generals, or other heroes of the Empire.

In 1887 Queen Victoria celebrated 50 years as queen, her Golden Jubilee. Masses of commemorative objects were made for people to buy. Mugs, cups and plates (source 16) linked loyalty to the Queen with pride in Britain and the Empire. Tea and table cloths showed the flags of the countries of the Empire alongside pictures of the royal family and the army and navy.

activity

2 Look at sources 14, 15 and 16.
a How do they show that people were interested in and proud of the Army, the Navy, Britain and the Empire?
b How did they help to increase that interest and pride?
3 Look at the information in the text. Cigarette cards made people:
a interested in
b proud of the Empire. How did they do this?

SOURCE 16

A plate commemorating Queen Victoria's Golden Jubilee in 1887. Find:

- Queen Victoria and her eldest son, Edward, the Prince of Wales.
- The map of the world with the Empire coloured red.
- Badges of countries of the Empire.
- Empire scenes.
- The clock with the words 'The Empire on which the sun never sets.' People were proud of saying this. It was always daytime in one country or another of the Empire.
- The names of various places in the Empire round the clock.
- The Latin motto *Ubi Virtus, ibi Victoria*, 'Where there is virtue, there is Victoria.' 'Victoria' is also the Latin word for victory.

assignments

1 Use the sources and information on pages 56–58 and in Part 3, pages 26–27.
a Make a list of the main ways in which the pattern of Britain's trade changed between 1750 and 1900, and write a few sentences about each one.
b Say what, if anything, stayed the same.

2 This is the start of a chart to show the various effects of the Empire on the British people, and which group was most affected in each case.
a Copy it out.
b Use the sources and information on pages 61–65 to help you to fill it in. Do this in as much detail as you can.
c Is it true that the Empire affected everyone in Britain in the same way? Give reasons for your answer and explain each one as fully as possible.

Effect	Affected mainly working class people	Affected mainly middle class people	Affected everybody
Opportunity to emigrate	✓		
Jobs abroad as administrators, doctors etc.		✓	
Cheaper butter and cheese			✓

3 Use the sources and information in Part 2, Part 3, pages 26–27, Part 4 and Part 5.
a What were the links between the Industrial Revolution and the development of the British Empire?
b Do you think that one was more important than the other in affecting the lives of ordinary people living in Britain? Give reasons for your answer and explain each one as fully as possible.

6

Images of Empire

The first section of Part 6 deals with the idea that the British Empire was valuable because it took the benefits of European civilisation to the backward native peoples of the colonies. You will see how historians have changed their opinions about this.

The second section shows how the Indian Mutiny and Rebellion has been portrayed since 1857 and examines some of the different explanations put forward about what happened.

The benefits of civilisation?

The mission to civilise

In the second half of the nineteenth century many British people became convinced that one of the main purposes of having an empire was to bring the benefits of European civilisation to the people whose lands they ruled. They believed the Empire gave them important responsibilities. In 1853 Earl Grey, the Colonial Secretary, said that he thought British rule was the most powerful way of:

SOURCE 1

Maintaining peace and order in many . . . regions of the earth . . .

Earl Grey, *The Colonial Policy of Lord John Russell's Administration*, 1853

And he believed it helped to spread:

SOURCE 2

Amongst millions of the human race, the blessings of Christianity and civilisation.

Earl Grey, *The Colonial Policy of Lord John Russell's Administration*, 1853

The exploits of explorers and missionaries like David Livingstone (source 3) caught the imagination of the British people. Livingstone undertook three expeditions in the centre of Africa between 1852

SOURCE 3

A statue of David Livingstone in Edinburgh. Livingstone was a Scot who trained as a medical missionary with the London Missionary Society. In the course of his expeditions he crossed the Kalahari desert to reach the Zambezi river and the waterfall which he called 'Victoria Falls' after the Queen, and explored Lake Tanganyika.

activity

I Look at source 3 and the information in the text. What reasons might the people of Edinburgh have had for putting up a statue of David Livingstone?

and his death in 1873. His aim was to open up to missionaries an area which was so far unknown to Europeans. He inspired many people when he returned to Britain and talked about the importance of taking the three 'Cs' to Africa: 'Christianity, Commerce [trade] and Civilisation'.

Why did the British believe in their mission?

When the British came across native peoples in the mid-nineteenth century they were often shocked by their way of life which they described as 'backward' and 'primitive'. As you found out in Part 1, this was the time when the British began to believe that mass production and trade could bring comfort and prosperity to the world. They believed they had a duty to improve the lives of people who did not know about modern technology and did not possess manufactured goods.

The British also found that native peoples were not Christians. They believed they had a duty to spread Christianity and to help people to live by its teachings.

Missionaries such as David Livingstone knew that there were still people who traded in slaves in Africa. They wanted to stop this because they believed it was against Christian teachings. They also wanted to help the people of Africa who had suffered when the British had traded in slaves in the eighteenth century. They believed the best way to do this was to teach them about Christianity, help to educate them, and enable them to buy British manufactured goods.

Attitudes towards native peoples

The British thought that to be civilised was to be like themselves. They thought civilised people were those that followed a similar way of life and held similar beliefs.

When the British came across native peoples who lived in different ways and held different beliefs they described them as 'uncivilised', and they felt superior to them. This attitude began to affect the way they viewed other races. The idea grew up that because native peoples lived in a different way, they were inferior to Europeans. This developed into a belief that the white races of the world were superior to the rest:

SOURCE 4

Left to himself and without white control and guidance, he [the black person] forgets the lessons he has learnt and slides rapidly back to his original barbarism.

Blackwoods Magazine, 1866

activity

2 G. A. Henty believed that white people were superior to black people and that the Empire helped to civilise black people.
a How do sources 5 and 6 reflect his own opinions?
b How do you think they helped to spread those opinions?
3 Look at source 7.
a Basil Davidson says 'Britain . . . became racist . . .' How do sources 4, 5 and 6 support that statement?
b Look at the information on pages 67–68. Why do you think he adds, 'though of course with the very best of intentions . . .'?

This idea grew and became widespread. By the end of the century it appeared in children's books. The typical view of black people was expressed by a character in one of G. A. Henty's stories for boys:

SOURCE 5

They are just like children. They are always either laughing or quarrelling. They are good-natured and passionate, indolent [lazy], but will work hard for a time; clever up to a certain point, densely stupid beyond. The intelligence of the average negro is about equal to that of a European child of ten years old.

G. A. Henty, *By Sheer Pluck*, 1884

Henty made him go on to say that, living among white people, black people gain:

SOURCE 6

A considerable amount of civilization. Left to their own devices, they retrograde [go backwards] into a state little above their native savagery.

G. A. Henty, *By Sheer Pluck*, 1884

Today we know that all these statements are wrong and that some races are not superior to others. But from the 1850s these ideas affected the attitudes of the British and helped to convince them that they should 'civilise' native peoples:

SOURCE 7

Britain in its age of power – from the mid-19th century – became racist, though of course with the very best of intentions, and would so remain for almost 100 years until the imperial power was spent [came to an end].

Basil Davidson, *Into the Dark Continent*, 1972

Native art and architecture

The belief that native peoples were uncivilised and inferior to Europeans meant that most British people knew little and understood even less about the artistic achievements of other peoples in the Empire. They thought of them as 'savages' and would have agreed with the novelist **Charles Dickens** who wrote:

i Charles Dickens

Charles Dickens (1812–70) started by writing sketches of London life and became the most popular writer of his time. His many novels, which include Oliver Twist (1838), David Copperfield (1850), Hard Times (1854) and Great Expectations (1861) contain vivid descriptions of all aspects of mid-nineteenth century life.

SOURCE 8

It is all one to me whether he [a savage] sticks . . . bits of trees through the lobes of his ears, or birds' feathers in his head . . . He is a savage – cruel, false, thievish, murderous . . .

Quoted in B. Hillier, *The Mask of Savagery*, 1973

Even so, some people did recognise that the peoples of the Empire had their own cultures, and took an interest in them. Many British visitors to India were fascinated by the art and architecture they saw there. The domes and painted arches of buildings such as the Taj Mahal (source 9) were copied in Britain (source 10).

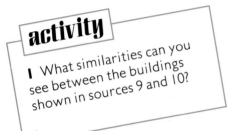

activity

1 What similarities can you see between the buildings shown in sources 9 and 10?

SOURCE 9

The Taj Mahal. After the death of his wife, Mumtaz Mahal, in 1629, the Mughal emperor Shah Jahan ordered it to be built to hold her body. It was designed by a Turkish architect and built between 1630 and 1648.

SOURCE 10

The Royal Pavilion, built in Brighton in 1817 for the Prince Regent, who became King George IV in 1820.

Some explorers and governors were interested in the customs, art, architecture and history of the peoples they encountered. Captain Cook, for example – who between 1768 and 1779 sailed to Tahiti and explored islands in the Pacific Ocean, the coasts of Australia and New Zealand – took careful notes of everything he saw.

Sir Stamford Raffles was Lieutenant Governor of Java during a brief period of British rule there between 1811 and 1816. He treated the Javanese with respect and took a lot of trouble to learn about their history. He also collected Javanese plants, stuffed animals, insects, carvings, writings, musical instruments and puppets (source 11). He returned to England with 200 boxes of material weighing nearly 30 tonnes.

SOURCE 11

Javanese shadow puppets from the collection of Sir Stamford Raffles. After his death his collection passed to the British Museum.

The first British governor of Fiji, Sir Arthur Gordon, also showed great respect for the Fijian people. He decorated his dining room with:

SOURCE 12

Spears and clubs, and great bowls, and native cloth. The house is so thoroughly in keeping with the country: so infinitely preferable to any attempt at making a Europeanised 'Governing House'.

C. F. Gordon Cumming, *At Home in Fiji*, late nineteenth century

activity

2a How can you tell from source 12 that Sir Arthur Gordon respected the Fijian people?

b Do you think Charles Dickens (source 8) would have agreed with him?

activity

1 Look at source 13. What effect do you think the British had on the Fijians' attitude to their own art and crafts?
2 Look at sources 11 and 14. Many British people thought native peoples could not produce anything of artistic value. Were they right?
3 Look at source 15 and the information in the text.
a How was the writer wrong?
b Why do you think he made this mistake?

Unfortunately, contact with the British caused the islanders to sell:

SOURCE 13

Their own admirable ornaments and wear instead trashy English necklaces.

C. F. Gordon Cumming, *At Home in Fiji*, late nineteenth century

SOURCE 14

A queen mother's head made out of bronze in sixteenth-century Benin. Bronze is a mixture of copper and tin. The artist made a wax model and covered it with clay. The wax was then melted away, and the clay used as a mould. Molten bronze was poured into it. When the bronze had hardened, the clay mould was broken off.

Despite the evidence of their long artistic traditions (source 14) the British continued to look upon African peoples, in particular, as uncivilised and inferior until well into the twentieth century. In the *New Empire Annual*, launched by the *Boys' Own Paper* in the 1930s, an article described the famous ruins of the ancient city of Zimbabwe in what was then known as Southern Rhodesia. The writer explained they were 3,000 years old and probably built by a vanished white people. He said:

SOURCE 15

There are no natives today living in South Africa who could have erected such monumental structures. The blacks possess nothing but little huts made of wood and boughs.

M. Marshall (ed.), *The New Empire Annual*, 1934

In fact, by 1928 archaeologists knew that the city almost certainly had been built at some time during the European Middle Ages by local Africans. More recent research has confirmed this.

Changing interpretations

For more than fifty years twentieth-century historians agreed with the nineteenth-century view that the British Empire brought the benefits of European civilisation to native peoples. A typical school textbook written in the 1950s said:

SOURCE 16

The Europeans have brought civilisation to the peoples of tropical Africa, whose standard of living has, in most cases, been raised as a result of their contact with white peoples.

J. Stembridge, *The World*, 1956

The author explained later in the book, that under the guidance of Europeans:

SOURCE 17

Roads and railways are being built and air routes are being extended. Doctors and scientists are working to improve the health of the Africans, who, on their part, are increasing in numbers; missionaries and teachers are educating the people.

J. Stembridge, *The World*, 1956

By the 1970s most countries of the Empire had become independent of Britain, some after bitter wars. British historians no longer looked at the Empire purely from the British or European point of view. A. J. P. Taylor pointed out that British rule did not necessarily benefit the peoples of the Empire:

SOURCE 18

Perhaps the subject peoples would have found a way of life more suited to their needs if they had been left to themselves. They were given no choice.

A. J. P. Taylor, *The Balance Sheet of Empire*, 1973

He pointed out that:

SOURCE 19

If European civilisation . . . be accepted as superior to African and Asian, then the British Empire was clearly a good thing. It depends on the point of view.

A. J. P. Taylor, *The Balance Sheet of Empire*, 1973

activity

I Do you think
a Stembridge (sources 16–17)
b Taylor (sources 18–20)
c Davidson (sources 21–23)
thought the British Empire was good or bad for Africa? Explain your reasons.

And he added:

SOURCE 20

Anyone who regards industrialisation and pollution and nuclear weapons as evil may regret that they are now spread throughout the world. That is what the British Empire helped to do.

A. J. P. Taylor, *The Balance Sheet of Empire*, 1973

In a school textbook written shortly afterwards, Basil Davidson said the British and other European empires did bring some benefits to Africa:

SOURCE 21

African civilisations needed to modernise themselves . . . the colonial system . . . sometimes did a little towards that. Many of the European colonial officials worked with a sincere devotion for the benefit of their 'subjects'.

Basil Davidson, *Discovering Africa's Past*, 1978

He said that many Africans came to prefer the fair way justice was handed out in some of the colonies to the sometimes unfair and unpredictable way in which their own rulers had governed them. Also, some Africans benefited from the introduction of a modern system of education, but:

SOURCE 22

Even this small amount of education was given in lessons which taught Africans that they were inferior to Europeans.

Basil Davidson, *Discovering Africa's Past*, 1978

The main problem, he went on, was that foreign companies often made big profits in a colony but then took the money. That meant the money could not be used to help the Africans living there, even though they had helped to earn it. Basil Davidson concluded that:

SOURCE 23

The blessings of European civilisation that were given to Africans during the colonial period were few and far between: and they were paid for at a high price.

Basil Davidson, *Discovering Africa's Past*, 1978

The Indian Mutiny and Rebellion, 1857–59

The events

In May 1857 Indian troops mutinied at Meerhut, near Delhi. They were angry with the British for many reasons which had built up over several years. The most recent reason was religious. The troops felt their beliefs were being ignored and they were being made to go against their religion.

There were two main religious groups in India, Hindus and Muslims. The Hindus believed the cow was a sacred animal. The Muslims believed pigs to be unclean. This meant that they could not touch products made from these animals.

In 1857 the British gave the soldiers a new type of cartridge to use in their rifles. It was coated with a grease made up of pork and beef fat and the soldiers had to bite each cartridge to prepare it for loading. Because of their religion both Hindus and Muslims refused to do this. When the British punished some of them by putting them in prison, the rest mutinied.

The mutineers captured Delhi and proclaimed their own emperor. Some Indian troops remained loyal to the British; others joined the mutiny. In some parts of India civilians from nearly all classes of the population also rose in rebellion. For a few months it looked as though the rebels might succeed, but after some desperate fighting the British managed to defeat the last of them in 1859.

How the events have been portrayed

The events of 1857 shocked the British, particularly the stories that soon arrived in Britain of terrible atrocities carried out by the Indians. At Cawnpore, for example, about two hundred British, mainly women and children, were massacred by an angry mob. For this the British blamed the local leader, Nana Sahib (source 24).

Paintings of the uprising by British artists also helped to shape the reaction of the British public. They concentrated mainly on the battles to put down the rebellion, and on the suffering and bravery of Christian women and children (source 25).

In the 1950s textbooks still told the story the way the British public heard it at the time. *The House of History*, for instance,

SOURCE 24

Nana Sahib. The British living in Cawnpore believed him to be friendly, but when the revolt began in 1857 he took the lead in his region. When the British regained control, he escaped to Nepal where he is thought to have died some years later.

SOURCE 25

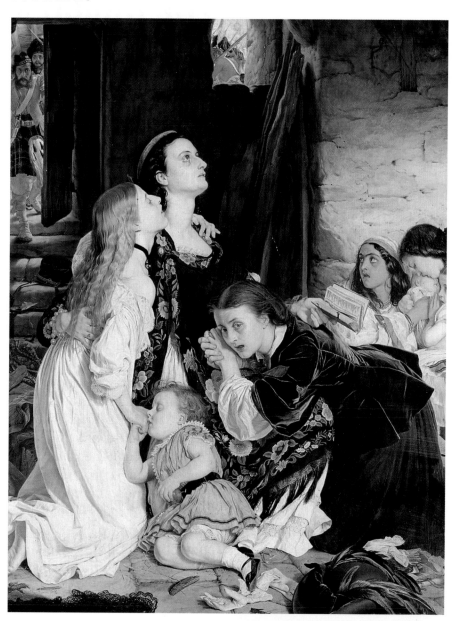

'In Memoriam', painted by Sir Joseph Noel Paton in 1858. It was 'Designed to Commemorate the Christian Heroism of the British Ladies in India during the Mutiny of 1857 and their ultimate Deliverance by British Prowess'. In his first version of the picture Noel Paton painted Indian mutineers bursting through the door, but he was persuaded to change them to Highland troops coming to the rescue.

activity

1 Look at source 25. Why do you think people wanted the artist to change his original picture?

originally written in the 1930s, was still being used in schools. The author described Indian atrocities in detail and went on:

SOURCE 26

After the Mutiny was quelled, the governor showed great mercy . . . The heroism of the recapture of Delhi, the tragedy of Cawnpore, and the long defence of Lucknow will never be forgotten.

Muriel Masefield, *The House of History, Third Storey*, 1931

activity

2 Look at sources 26, 27 and 28.
a What do Bayly and Porter say about the events that Masefield does not?
b People who tell stories or write books have a purpose – to get at the truth, make people laugh, etcetera. What do you think
(i) Masefield and
(ii)Bayly
are trying to do?

Today, accounts of the events also include the atrocities carried out by the British:

SOURCE 27

Indians were shot and hanged out of hand, burned alive, and blown from guns by the British. In their turn the rebels massacred British women and children.

B. Porter, *The Lion's Share*, 1975

SOURCE 28

In reality Indian atrocities often followed news of outrages committed by British troops, or were equalled by them. The famous massacre of . . . Cawnpore, for instance, was matched by General Neill's execution of civilians in nearby districts.

C. A. Bayly, *The Raj, India and the British 1600–1947*, 1990

Mutiny, rebellion or nationalist uprising?

Once the Mutiny and Rebellion had been put down the British in India started to argue about why it had happened. British administrators immediately blamed the army and claimed the uprising was simply a mutiny which happened because British officers were insensitive to Indian beliefs and feelings. Army officers blamed the administrators for angering civilians and claimed the revolt involved civilians just as much as soldiers.

Historians still argue about this today. Until the 1960s British historians argued that the uprising was purely military and, as a result, school textbooks took this line too:

SOURCE 29

The Mutiny was not a rising of the Indian people but only of the sepoys [Indian soldiers] of the Bengal army . . . this was probably because there were many races in India, some of which hated one another much more than they disliked the British.

G. W. Southgate, *An Introduction to English History*, Books I–III, 1947

Today, both Indian and British historians agree that the uprising involved both the army and many members of the civilian population. That is why many historians no longer write of the 'Indian Mutiny' but of the 'Indian Mutiny and Rebellion' or the 'Indian Rebellion'. Most British historians believe civilians had a variety of motives for rebelling, and that sometimes they also fought against each other for particular local reasons.

SOURCE 30

activity

1 Look at source 30. What effect do you think the lack of Indian pictures of the events of 1857–59 has had on historians' explanations of what happened? Why?

2 Look at source 32. Why do you think
a British officials and
b Indian officials took the actions they did to commemorate the siege of the British Residency at Lucknow?

Rani Lakshmi Bai of Jhansi, painted in 1930. The Rani of Jhansi was killed leading fighting against the British in 1858. She became an Indian heroine of the revolt and a symbol of armed resistance to British rule. There are very few Indian pictures of the rebellion because the British put it down so firmly. Pictures of the Rani were first paraded in public by Indian nationalists around 1900.

In 1947 the British left India, which was divided into the two independent countries of India and Pakistan. Many Indian and Pakistani writers interpret the events of 1857 as more than a rebellion. They describe them as a 'nationalist movement', that is, a movement that united people of all classes in India in an attempt to get rid of the British (source 30). This view is:

SOURCE 31

The official view propagated [given out] on television and radio in India and Pakistan today.

C. A. Bayly, *The Raj, India and the British 1600–1947*, 1990

The events of 1857 are of great importance to the people of India today, as this story shows. When the uprising began in 1857, all the Europeans and Christians in the town of Lucknow took refuge in the British Residency. Guarded by a few loyal Indian troops, they were besieged there by the rebels for several months. Finally a column of troops fought their way through to relieve them.

By this time the Residency had been more or less destroyed. But it mattered so much to the British to have recaptured it that they kept the Union Jack flying over the ruins until midnight on the day of Indian Independence in 1947. With the British gone, the Indians were free to put up their own memorial. The Union Jack was:

SOURCE 32

Replaced by a plaque commemorating the thousands of Indians who died in the siege, trying to free their country from foreign rule.

C. A. Bayly, *The Raj, India and the British 1600–1947*, 1990

assignments

1a Source 16 sees the British Empire as good for Africa. Look at sources 17, 19, 20 and 21 and the information in the text on pages 67–72. Make a list of the points which you think support this view.
b Source 23 disagrees. Look at sources 18, 19, 20, and 22 and the information in the text on pages 67–72. Make a list of the points which you think support this view.
c Explain what you think are (i) the strengths, (ii) the weaknesses of the different views put forward in source 16 and source 23.

2 Use the sources and information on pages 75–78. Muriel Masefield (see source 26 and the information in the text) gave what many people still believe to be an accurate account of the events of 1857–59.
a What did she leave out that is now known to have happened?
b Look at source 26. What do you think are (i) the strengths, (ii) the weaknesses of writing a school history textbook in this way?

3 For a long time British historians described the events of 1857–59 as a mutiny by Indian soldiers which did not involve civilians at all. What reasons for this are suggested by
a the attitude of British administrators (see page 77)
b source 30?

4a Look at the sources and information on pages 77–78. What explanation of the events of 1857–59 is (i) favoured by most British historians, (ii) given out as the official view by Indian and Pakistani radio and television?
b The official view is the view of the governments of India and Pakistan. Why do you think they are likely to prefer that explanation?

7

Parliament and Protest

In Parts 2, 3 and 4 you found out about some of the great changes which took place in Britain between 1750 and 1900. As well as affecting people's home and working lives, the changes also altered their attitude to Parliament. Many people came to believe that Members of Parliament were out of touch with their needs. Part 7 is about how Parliament itself was changed as a result of this discontent, and how various groups continued to protest because they believed the changes did not go far enough. You will be able to investigate what some of these groups wanted and whether or not they achieved their aims.

The Great Reform Act, 1832

In 1832 Parliament passed a law which changed the arrangements about which places could elect a Member of Parliament (MP) to represent them. It also changed the rules about who could vote in Parliamentary elections. These were the first big changes of this kind ever made. The law has been known ever since as 'The Great Reform Act'.

SOURCE 1

Constituency	Number of MPs
English county	2
Welsh county	1
Scottish county	1
English borough	2
Welsh borough	2
Scottish borough	1 between 4 boroughs

Counties and Boroughs, and the MPs they sent to Parliament.

What the Act said

Constituencies

A 'constituency' is the area of the country which an MP represents in Parliament. MPs were sent to Parliament by two different kinds of constituency, counties and boroughs. Source 1 shows how many MPs they elected. Boroughs had been given their rights in the Middle Ages when they were busy seaports or market towns. By 1831 many of them became known as 'rotten boroughs', (source 2), because they had tiny populations and were no longer

SOURCE 2

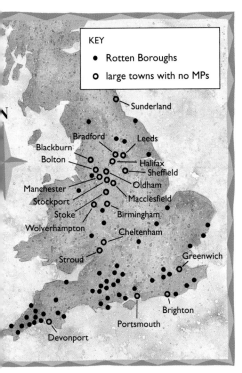

Parliamentary representation in 1831 in England. As a result of the 1832 Reform Act, all the large towns shown without MPs became Parliamentary boroughs and all the rotten boroughs were abolished.

important places. Appelby in Cumbria, for example, had only one voter and Bramber in Sussex was a tiny village. Yet they still had the right to elect two MPs (source 2).

Meanwhile new big towns such as Manchester, Leeds Birmingham and Bradford were not represented at all. It was obvious that the way Parliamentary seats (places in the House of Commons) were distributed around the country in 1831 did not reflect the changes that had taken place in the size of the population and in where people actually lived (see Part 2, source 1).

The Act of 1832 changed this. 143 MPs were taken away from those parts of the country which had too many MPs (such as Cornwall) and given to those that did not have enough (such as Lancashire). Extra MPs were also given to Scotland and Ireland because they had the least seats.

Who could vote

Both before and after 1832 the right to vote depended on how much property a man owned (source 3). Women could not vote at all. Before the 1832 Act one adult (over 21) man in ten could vote; after it, one adult man in five. The new voters were the fairly well-off tenant farmers in the countryside, and the middle classes in the towns, together with a very few of the better-off among the working classes.

SOURCE 3

<table>
<tr><td rowspan="2">Counties or Boroughs</td><td colspan="2">Qualifications for voters</td></tr>
<tr><td>Before 1832</td><td>After 1832</td></tr>
<tr><td>Counties</td><td>Male owners of freehold land or property valued for the land tax at least £2 per year. This meant men who owned large farms.</td><td>1 Male owners of freehold land or property valued for the land tax at least £2 per year.
2 Men who payed at least £50 a year in rent for their land. This meant well-off tenant farmers.</td></tr>
<tr><td>Boroughs</td><td>Varied between every adult man and one man in a hundred according to the ancient rights and customs of each borough.</td><td>All adult men living in property worth at least £10 a year in rent. This meant the middle classes and a very few of the better-off among the working classes.</td></tr>
</table>

Voting qualifications before and after the 1832 Reform Act.

activity

1 Look at source 2, the information in the text and source 2 in Part 2. Explain in what ways the system of Parliamentary representation was out of date in 1831.
2 Look at source 2 and the information in the text. Which parts of the country
a lost
b gained MPs as a result of the 1832 Reform Act?

Who wanted reform?

Working class people had lived through hard times since the end of a long period of war with France in 1815. Prices were high, especially the price of bread, and many people could not find jobs. Many of them believed that their lives would improve if they had the vote. They thought this would give them the power to elect people to Parliament who cared about making things better for them.

SOURCE 4

The massacre at Peterloo in 1819, a cartoon drawn by George Cruikshank. Henry Hunt was speaking to a crowd of 60,000 men, women and children at St Peter's Field in Manchester when the magistrates ordered a volunteer force of cavalry to arrest him. They rode into the crowd and lost control. Eleven people were killed and hundreds seriously injured. The event was mockingly called 'Peterloo' after the British victory over the French at Waterloo four years earlier.

They attended big open air meetings to hear speakers such as Henry Hunt, a Wiltshire farmer, who believed the political system had to be changed (source 3). They read the writings of William Cobbett:

SOURCE 5

It will be asked, will the reform of Parliament give the labouring man a cow or a pig, will it put bread and cheese into his satchel instead of infernal cold potatoes . . . and I answer distinctly that it would do them all.

William Cobbett, *Political Register*, 1832

Cobbett believed that reform would make a real difference to the comfort and prosperity of working people because MPs would have to take more notice of them once they had the vote.

Middle-class businessmen and factory owners wanted reform because their cities were unrepresented. They wanted MPs who understood the needs of business and industry:

SOURCE 6

That honourable House [of Commons], in its present state, is ... too far removed in habits [way of life], wealth and station [position], from the wants [needs] and interests of the lower and middle classes of people, to have ... any close identity of feeling with them. The great aristocratical interests of all kinds are well represented there ... But the interests of Industry and of Trade have scarcely any representatives at all!

Declaration of the Birmingham Political Union, 1829

Who opposed reform?

Many big landowners opposed reform because they were worried about losing power. The land and property they owned meant they could often dictate who should be returned to Parliament in a particular county or borough.

Others opposed reform because they were afraid new voters might use their vote to overturn the old way of doing things. They believed the existing system worked and should not be altered in case it made things worse rather than better. They were frightened of the crowds of people who met to demand reform.

How the Reform Bill was passed

Earl Grey, Leader of the Whig party and the Government, was convinced of the need for reform. He believed that business people should be represented. He was worried because a fall in trade had created high unemployment and low wages. This had already led to popular unrest. Grey was also worried that revolution would break out as it just had in France. All the same, he did not intend to give the working classes the vote.

Grey put his ideas for Reform to Parliament but there were not enough Whig MPs to support him. In order to gain more support Grey persuaded the King to dissolve Parliament and call a General Election. Many reformers were elected and Grey then had a majority of 130 MPs. His reforms were passed by the House of Commons. However, the House of Lords refused to support them.

When people heard the news, riots broke out (source 6). Grey tried again but the Lords still refused to support him. Grey asked the King to create 50 new Lords. The King refused and Grey resigned. However, the Tory party could not form a Government and so the King asked Grey to remain in government and agreed to make as many new Lords as he needed. The threat was enough. The reforms were passed by the Lords and became known as the Great Reform Act of 1832.

activity

1 Use the sources and information on pages 82–83.
a Write a short speech by (i) a Tory lord opposing the Reform Bill, (ii) a factory owner supporting it.
b In the passing of the Reform Bill, what part do you think was played by fear of events (i) in England, (ii) abroad?

SOURCE 7

A painting of the Bristol Riots in Queen Square, October 1831.

Further Reform Acts

The 1832 Reform Act did not give the vote to the mass of the working class as they had hoped. Only a few very well-off workers qualified. The great majority of men and all women in Britain still had no right to vote. There were only 650,000 voters out of a total adult population of about 14 million. It took two further Reform Acts in the nineteenth century, and two in the twentieth, before this right was held by all adults, men and women (sources 8 and 9).

activity

I Use sources 8 and 9 and the information in the text.
a Which Reform Act increased the number of voters by the greatest percentage?
b Which Act do you think was the most important? Think about your reasons carefully and then discuss your ideas in a small group.
2 Use the sources and information on pages 80–84. Explain why you think the 1832 Reform Act is remembered as the 'Great' Reform Act.

SOURCE 8

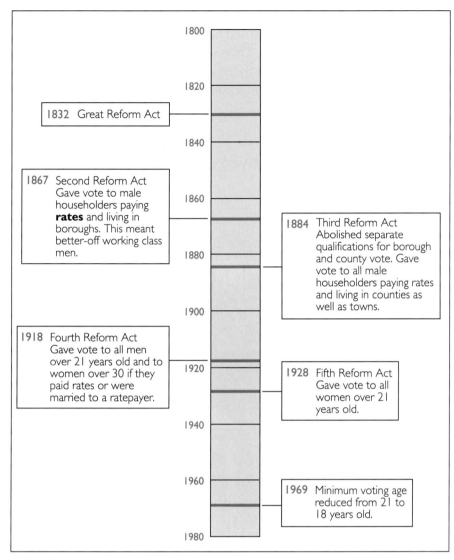

Parliamentary reform 1832–1969.

SOURCE 9

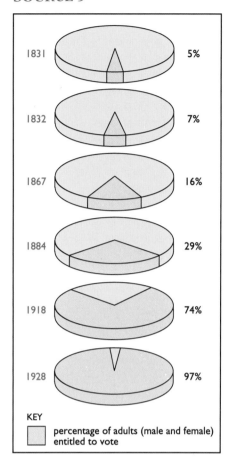

The approximate percentages of all male and female adults entitled to vote in various years. The figure for 1928 is 97 per cent rather than 100 per cent because all voters had to live in a place for six months before they qualified to be put on their local voting register. There were always some people waiting to qualify.

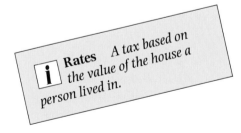

Rates A tax based on the value of the house a person lived in.

Political parties

After 1832 two political parties began to develop, the Liberals and the Conservatives. They were connected to the Whig and Tory parties which had grown up in the eighteenth century, but there were also important differences.

Whigs and Tories

The Whig and Tory parties were not like modern political parties at all. They were groups of members of the House of Commons and House of Lords, organised mainly around family links and personal friendships.

The important thing was that most MPs did not belong to either group. When there was a general election voters did not vote for a party as most do today. They voted for a particular individual to represent them in Parliament. They usually made their choice for local and personal reasons. So there were many independent MPs in the House of Commons who voted sometimes with the Whigs and sometimes with the Tories.

The Liberal and Conservative Parties

SOURCE 10

A Punch cartoon of 1870 showing the rival party leaders, Disraeli (left) and Gladstone (right).

After 1832 the Whigs became known as Liberals and the Tories as Conservatives. After the 1867 Reform Act there were many more new voters and both parties started to try to win them over at elections. In particular they set up national organisations to try to make sure their candidates were elected in each constituency.

Beginning in the 1860s the two great party leaders and rivals were William Gladstone (Liberal) and Benjamin Disraeli (Conservative). The Liberals were mainly supported by old Whig landowning families, businessmen from the new industrial towns, professional people such as doctors and lawyers, **nonconformists** and many working-class people. The Tories also appealed to working-class voters but their strongest support came from members of the Church of England and country gentlemen.

> **ℹ Nonconformists**
> Nonconformists were also known as Dissenters. They were Protestants who did not accept the Church of England. They included groups such as the Independents, Baptists and Quakers, which had grown up in the seventeenth century, and the Methodists, founded by John Wesley in the eighteenth century.

The Chartists

Throughout the nineteenth century, many people found that despite reforms and changes, Parliament was not able to respond to their needs. In the case studies that follow you will be able to investigate three movements formed by people who were not satisfied with Parliament. The first of these is the Chartists. What did they want and did they achieve their aims?

The Charter

The Chartists were the supporters of 'The People's Charter', which made six demands for the reform of Parliament. It was written by a cabinet maker called William Lovett and supported at a large rally held in Birmingham in 1838. The Charter demanded:

1 *A vote* for every man over 21 who was sane and not in prison.

2 *The secret ballot.* People were to vote in secret, without fear of what might happen to them afterwards.

3 *No property qualification* for Members of Parliament. This would abolish the rule that anyone wishing to become an MP had to own a lot of property. It would then be possible for poor men to become MPs.

4 *Payment of Members of the House of Commons.* MPs were unpaid. Poor men could not afford to become MPs unless they were paid.

5 *Equal constituencies.* Each constituency was to have the same number of people in it. This would give places of the same size the same number of MPs and therefore the same amount of power.

6 *Annual Parliaments.* In the 1830s there could be up to seven years between elections. Many people still tried to bribe their way into Parliament. Elections every year would make it too expensive to do this. Also MPs would have to pay more attention to the opinions of the voters if they had to face an election annually.

The Charter was supported by both men and women. Some people wanted women to have the vote too. They suggested 'votes for women' should be a seventh point on the Charter but this did not become official policy. Women took part in Chartist meetings and joined women's associations which tried to find ways in which women could support their sons and husbands.

Why did people support the Charter?

Belief in Parliament

You found out in Parts 2 and 4 that the growth of cities meant that many working-class people lived in unhealthy houses in filthy streets. They often worked very long hours in factories in dangerous conditions. Their wages were low and they could be put out of work if the demand for what they were making suddenly dropped.

Most working people wanted a better life and believed that Parliament had the power to change things for the better. That is why they wanted the vote. They wanted to be able to elect MPs who knew what their lives were like and would do something to improve them.

The editor of the *Leicester Chronicle* wrote that Chartism meant:

SOURCE 11

Better wages, limited hours of labour, comfort, independence, happiness . . .

Quoted in P. Searby, *The Chartists*, 1989

Disappointment with the 1832 Reform Act

The working classes were bitterly disappointed with the 1832 Reform Act. They had believed they would win the right to vote and would, therefore, be able to choose MPs who would have their interests at heart.

In fact, the Whigs made sure that the Reform Act excluded nearly all working-class people from the right to vote. Almost all of the new voters were owners of small properties such as farmers and shopkeepers. Also, MPs still mainly represented landowners.

Working-class people felt betrayed. They were all the more determined to support further changes that would give them proper representation in Parliament.

Poverty and unemployment

Many working people's lives were even harder than usual in the late 1830s and the 1840s. During these years there were several periods of industrial 'depression', times when manufacturers found it hard to sell their goods. That meant some workers were given lower wages while many lost their jobs altogether. When the depressions were at their worst (in 1839, 1842 and 1848) the largest number of people supported the Chartists.

SOURCE 12

The Pass Room at Bridewell Workhouse Women came here before they were sent to the wards in the workhouse.

The New Poor Law

In the 1830s very poor people, the unemployed and the sick were still looked after under the Poor Law Act of 1601. They received a small amount of money each week from their parish's 'poor relief' fund. The money came from householders in the parish who had to pay a tax called a 'rate' (see page 85).

The number of people asking for poor relief grew in the early nineteenth century. In 1775 the amount needed for poor relief was less than £2 million: in 1831 it was nearly £7 million. The ratepayers complained that this was too much.

Parliament agreed. In 1834 it passed the Poor Law Amendment Act which changed the system in order to reduce costs. Parishes were grouped together into Poor Law Unions. Each Union was expected to set up a workhouse (source 12) where nearly everyone receiving poor relief had to live and work. Workhouses were to be made as unpleasant as possible so that poor people would not want to go there. This would save money. One official said the idea behind workhouses was:

SOURCE 13

To make them a terror to the poor and prevent them from entering.

Quoted in P. Searby, *The Chartists*, 1989

The old system had offered help in times of trouble; the new system appeared to be designed to punish people for their misfortunes. All working-class people hated it. They felt insulted and angry at the thought of their families having to go into what seemed like a prison.

Working people wanted the New Poor Law repealed (cancelled) and this added to their determination to be represented in Parliament. At Chartist meetings banners called for the end of the New Poor Law and speakers attacked the 'headless, brutal, brainless Poor Law Commissioners' who had recommended the new scheme in the first place.

Violence or peaceful persuasion?

All Chartists agreed that a petition should be sent to Parliament asking for the Charter to be made law. They disagreed about what to do if Parliament rejected this. Some were in favour of using violence if necessary; others believed strongly that the only way forward was by trying to persuade MPs peacefully.

The supporters of violence were strongest in places where there were large numbers of handloom weavers facing low wages and unemployment (see Part 4, page 49).

activity

I Use the sources and information on pages 89–90.

a Two Chartists are discussing the rights and wrongs of using physical force to achieve their aims. One supports its use, the other does not. Write out the argument that you think they might have.

b From what you have found out about the Chartists, do you agree with George Cruikshank's ideas in source 15? Give your reasons.

Those who believed in persuasion were usually skilled craftspeople such as shoemakers, tailors, printers and cabinet-makers. William Lovett, the author of the Charter, came from this group. He wrote:

SOURCE 14

Muskets are not what is wanted, but education and schooling of the working people . . .

William Lovett, *Life and Struggles*, 1876

Petitions to Parliament

At first the Chartists used peaceful means, but each time they presented their Charter Parliament refused to consider it, even though by 1842 it was supported by a petition signed by three million people.

SOURCE 15

'A Commons Scene', a cartoon by George Cruikshank, showing what he thought the House of Commons would be like if the Six Points of the People's Charter ever became law.

Uprisings and riots

SOURCE 16

The Newport Rising, November 1839. John Frost, a former Mayor of Newport and a Chartist, led 7,000 miners and ironworkers on a march to take over Newport. They fought a brief battle with troops stationed at the Westgate Hotel. Fourteen Chartists were shot dead and 125 arrested, including Frost. He was sentenced to death but later transported to New South Wales instead. He was pardoned in 1854.

As soon as Parliament rejected the Chartists' first petition in 1839, violence broke out in South Wales (source 16) and in many towns in northern England and the midlands. However, as the commander of the troops sent to the north realised, the Chartists were never a serious threat to the government. He wrote in his diary:

SOURCE 17

Poor creatures, their threats of attack are miserable. With half a cartridge, and half a pike, with no money, no discipline, no skilful leaders, they would attack men with leaders, money and discipline, well armed and having sixty rounds a man. Poor men!

Sir Charles Napier's diary, 1 December 1839, quoted in Sir W. Napier,
Life and Opinions of General Sir Charles Napier, 1857

The next day he wrote:

SOURCE 18

The streets of this town are horrible. The poor starving people go about by twenties and forties, begging ... Nothing can exceed [be greater than] the good behaviour of these poor people, except [unless] it be their cruel sufferings!

Sir Charles Napier's diary, 2 December 1839, quoted in Sir W. Napier,
Life and Opinions of General Sir Charles Napier, 1857

activity

2 Look at sources 17 and 18.
a What evidence is there in them that General Napier (i) did, (ii) did not sympathise with the Chartists?
b How reliable do you think they are as evidence about (i) the Chartists (ii) General Napier's attitudes? Give your reasons.

activity

1 Look at source 19.
a What impression does it give you of the Chartist movement?
b How reliable do you think it is as evidence? Give your reasons.

Parliament's rejection of the Chartists' second petition in 1842 coincided with another severe depression in the midlands and north of England. Factory owners cut wages and the workers went on strike. They also managed to sabotage factories. Many, though not all, of the strikers were Chartists. Once again troops were called out and there were fights and arrests. Many strikers were imprisoned or transported.

The final petition, 1848

In 1847 a depression again put many people out of work. In 1848 the Chartist leader, Feargus O'Connor, announced that over six million people had signed a new petition. He planned a mass meeting on Kennington Common in London, followed by a march to present the petition to Parliament. He said 500,000 people would be there.

The governments of most European countries had been overthrown by revolutions that year. So the British government was worried. Ministers thought the Chartist rally might be the start of a revolution in Britain. They called in troops and extra police. The police asked O'Connor to hand the petition in on his own and he agreed.

Only about 20,000 people turned up to the rally which passed off peacefully (source 19). O'Connor took the petition to Parliament where officials read it and counted the signatures. They found that only two million were genuine. The rest were made up of names and forgeries. The petition became a joke. This allowed Parliament once again to ignore the Charter and its six demands. After that, Chartism died out.

SOURCE 19

An early photograph of the Chartist meeting on Kennington Common, 10 April 1848.

The Fenians

How did the Fenians begin?

Although Ireland and Britain shared the same monarch, there were two Parliaments, one in London covering England, Wales and Scotland, and one in Dublin covering Ireland. No Catholic could become an MP in either Parliament although the majority of the Irish population, both working and middle class, were Catholic.

However, as a result of English rule in Ireland in the sixteenth and seventeenth centuries, most landlords were Protestants. So the Catholics had no power or representation in Ireland at all.

In 1798 there was a rebellion by Catholic peasant farmers against their Protestant landlords. The British government's response was to pass the Act of Union which abolished the Irish Parliament. From 1801 Protestant Irish MP's were elected to the British Parliament in London.

The Irish Protestant landlords did not like losing their Irish Parliament which they controlled, but they had been frightened by the rebellion. The Irish Catholics in Ireland and Catholics in Britian, however, still had no representation in any Parliament. An Irish Catholic, Daniel O'Connell, led a successful campaign to change the law and from 1829 Catholics could become MPs. O'Connell was elected in 1830 and then campaigned to abolish the Act of Union in order to restore the Irish Parliament in Dublin, this time with both Catholic and Protestant MPs. The Tory government refused to make any changes and banned O'Connell's meetings (source 20).

SOURCE 20

A meeting at Tara in 1843 organised by O'Connell to protest against the Act of Union. It was attended by about 250,000 people.

activity

1 Use the sources and information on pages 93–94. Why do you think some Irish people decided that violence rather than the use of Parliament was the way to solve Ireland's problems with Britain?

O'Connell accepted this because he believed only in lawful and peaceful protest. This annoyed some of his supporters who believed the British government would never be persuaded to abolish the Act of Union unless it was forced to as a result of violent actions. A group called the Young Irelanders felt this way. They also believed that the only answer to Ireland's problems was to break away from British rule and become an independent country.

Then, between 1846 and 1848, Ireland was hit by the great potato famine (see Part 5, page 61). Those that survived blamed the British government for not doing enough to help. The British allowed Irish grain to be exported to Britain when it was desperately needed by starving people in Ireland, and they provided extra food too late.

In 1848 the Young Irelanders started a rebellion to try to achieve their aims but it failed. Two of the leaders, James Stephens and John O'Mahoney, had to leave Ireland to avoid arrest. They were determined to try again. Ten years later they founded new groups. Stephens founded the Irish Republican Brotherhood (IRB) in Dublin and O'Mahoney founded the Fenian brotherhood in the USA.

The members of both groups were known as the Fenians which came from Fienna, a legendary group of Irish warriors. All Fenians had the same aims: to overthrow British rule in Ireland by an armed uprising and set up a separate Irish Republic.

To avoid detection by the government the Fenians were organised as a secret society. Members had to take an oath of obedience to their superior officers. Source 21 shows you who supported the Fenians and who opposed them.

SOURCE 21

activity

2 Look at sources 20 and 21.
a What kind of people (i) supported (ii) opposed the Fenians?
b What were their reasons?
3 Look at source 22 and the information in the text on pages 95 and 96.
a Why do you think Colonel Kelly's plans failed?
b Do you think the Fenian Rising helped the Irish people in any way? Give your reasons.

Supporters	
Group	Reasons
Many groups especially poor Catholic tenant farmers	Blamed the British for not doing enough to help during the famine.
Irish emigrants in the USA who raised money to buy arms for an uprising	Also blamed the British for not doing enough to help during the famine.
Poor Catholic Irish tenants	Many were being evicted from their homes and land by Protestant landlords because they could not afford to pay the rent (source 22).

Opponents	
Group	Reasons
Protestants	Wanted to keep the Act of Union.
Irish MPs	Opposed use of violence rather than peaceful persuasion.
Catholic Bishops	Opposed secret societies bound by oaths. Feared the Fenians might attack the Church.
Middle class Catholics	Did not like violent protest. Feared that a successful Fenian uprising might lead to an attack on property owners such as themselves.

Supporters and opponents of the Fenians

SOURCE 22

A landlord evicting tenants in Ireland.

What did the Fenians achieve?

Although in many ways the Fenian movement was not a success, it did have some important results.

In 1866 Colonel Kelly who had fought in the American Civil War took over the leadership in Ireland from James Stephens. The Fenians needed arms so Kelly planned to capture an arms depot at Chester Castle in England and then follow this with an uprising in 1867. But the attack at Chester failed and the uprising was put off for a month. Spies told the government what was going on, so when the time came it was ready. Many leaders were arrested and the thousands of Fenians that turned out were scattered or captured by armed police.

Colonel Kelly was arrested in Manchester several months later. About thirty Fenians attacked the police van he was in, killed the sergeant guarding it, and rescued Kelly (source 23). Three men were tried and hanged for the murder of the sergeant. They became known as the Manchester Martyrs. Later in the year Fenians blew a hole in the wall of Clerkenwell prison in London in an attempt to free a colleague. The explosion killed twelve civilians and wounded several others.

SOURCE 23

Fenians rescuing Colonel Kelly in Manchester, Septmeber 1867.

i **Home Rule**   Gladstone's plan was to set up an Irish Parliament in Dublin to run Irish home affairs with the Parliament in London still in charge of foreign policy and trade.

These incidents in England made the British people feel that the Union with Ireland could affect their lives. William Gladstone, who became Prime Minister of a Liberal government in 1868, decided to take some positive actions to help the Irish people. 'My mission is to pacify (bring peace to) Ireland,' he announced.

Gladstone passed a law which meant that Catholics no longer had to pay a tithe, or tax, to the Protestant Church of Ireland. Also his Land Act gave some protection, though not enough, to tenants against landowners. He also tried to give the Irish **Home Rule** but he met too much opposition in the British Parliament.

The Fenian movement did not die out. Members of the Irish Republican Brotherhood kept their aims and became even more secretive. They became openly active again in 1913.

The creation of the Labour Party

Although the Reform Acts of 1867 and 1884 gave many working-class men the right to vote, very few of them became Members of Parliament. It was difficult for a working-class man to become an MP because MPs were still not paid at this time, and it cost a candidate a lot of money to take part in an election. The few that did go into the House of Commons were members of the Liberal Party.

In the 1890s people became convinced that a new party was needed, independent of both the Conservatives and the Liberals, to put up working-class candidates in elections. This eventually led to the formation of the Labour Party in 1906, but it was a slow process which would not have happened at all without the trade unions.

Socialists

Nineteenth-century socialists came mainly from middle-class backgrounds at first. They believed that society worked in an unfair way that left a large number of working-class people very poor and badly housed. They believed the only way to improve things for them was to change the system.

Instead of wealthy individuals owning things such as land, factories, and shops, socialists wanted the people to own them.

i Social Democratic Federation *Founded as the Democratic Foundation in 1881 it became the Social Democratic Foundation (SDF) in 1884. The SDF was led by H. M. Hyndman and had a mainly middle class membership. It was strong in London and organised unemployment demonstrations in 1886 and 1887.*

i Fabian Society *Founded in 1884. Its members were mainly middle class writers and thinkers based in London, such as George Bernard Shaw and Sidney Webb. Fabians aimed to create reform gradually by argument and persuasion, first through the Liberal Party and Later through the Independant Labour Party.*

In that way everybody would be able to share in the wealth they helped to create. They also wanted the government to help working people straight away, for example by setting up a system of state pensions, so that everyone would have money to live off in their old age.

There were several socialist organisations such as the **Social Democratic Federation** and the **Fabian Society**. By 1890 there were only 2,000 socialists altogether, but they were important because of the ideas they spread through their meetings and writing.

The Independent Labour Party

In the 1890s socialist ideas spread among working-class people in the north of England where many local socialist and labour clubs were formed. These groups wanted nothing to do with the Conservative and Liberal parties. In 1893 the Independent Labour Party (ILP) was formed after a conference held in Bradford.

Keir Hardie led the party. He was a working-class Scottish socialist who had formed the Scottish Labour Party in 1888. He had been elected as an independent labour MP for West Ham in 1892. Hardie believed a new Labour Party was needed in England to represent the working-class people in Parliament.

The ILP was particularly strong in the North. Its members felt passionately about their cause. Philip Snowden, who eventually became the first Labour Chancellor of the Exchequer, helped to spread their ideas. Later he remembered:

SOURCE 22

It was an inspiration . . . Socialism to those men and women was a new vision.

Philip Snowden, *An Autobiography*, 1934

Merrie England, a popular book on socialism, became a best seller:

SOURCE 23

I would have public parks, public theatres, music halls, gymnasiums, football and cricket fields, public halls and public gardens for recreation and music and refreshment. I would have all our children fed and clothed and educated at the cost of the State.

Robert Blatchford, *Merrie England*, 1894

Despite all this energy, all 28 ILP candidates, including Keir Hardie, were defeated in the 1895 general election. It was clear that they would need more money to organise themselves into a mass socialist party. Hardie believed the answer was for socialists to work with trade unionists. This did happen but was not inevitable.

activity

I What do source 23 and the information in the text tell you about:
a The new responsibilities which socialists wanted the government to have?
b Why working class people might have began to support socialist ideas?

Trade unions

Model unions

Many workers joined the Chartist movement in the 1840s in the hope of winning the vote so that they could be properly represented in Parliament. When this failed, many skilled workers turned to trade unions as a way of improving their lives. By the 1870s skilled craftspeople such as carpenters, textile workers, coal miners, engineers and bricklayers had succeeded in forming strong unions that were accepted by both employers and the government.

These 'model unions', as they were known, such as the Amalgamated Society of Joiners and Carpenters and the

SOURCE 24

A membership certificate of the Amalgamated Society of Engineers, founded in 1851. The pictures show some of the things made by the workers in the union. The portraits include two of the first engineers, James Watt (see page 36) and Richard Arkwright (see page 45).

activity

1 How does source 24 suggest that members of this union **a** thought their skills were important to other people **b** felt proud of them?

2 Look at source 25

a what impression does it give of the Dock Strike?

b How reliable do you think it is?

Amalgamated Society of Engineers (source 24), were national organisations that brought together what had previously been local craft associations. They were expensive to join and only well-paid skilled workers could afford the subscriptions. In return they provided important benefits such as unemployment pay, sick pay and old age pensions.

New unions

The great majority of workers, the unskilled ones, did not belong to the model unions. In the 1880s they began to form their own 'new unions'. The new unions had low subscriptions and aimed to improve their members' pay and working conditions. Unlike the old craft unions, they were prepared to take strike action.

In 1888 the matchgirl workers at Bryant and May's factory in London formed a union and held a successful strike for better wages and conditions of work. In 1889 London gas workers formed a union and used the threat of a strike to win the right to work only eight hours a day. Later in 1889 the London dock workers went on strike to persuade employers to pay them 6d (2.5p) per day (source 25).

These strikes were well organised and peaceful and made the public realise how very poor and badly paid most unskilled workers were. They also helped to increase union membership. In four years, between 1888 and 1892, it grew from 750,000 to 1.5 million.

SOURCE 25

Dock workers voting during their strike in 1889.

activity

3 Look at sources 24, 25 and the information in the text.
a What kind of workers belonged to (i) the model unions (ii) the new unions?
b Make a list of reasons why you think that before 1899 (i) the model unions opposed the TUC setting up a separate organisation to send independent working class representatives to Parliament (ii) the new unions supported it.

i Trades Union Congress The Trades Union Congress was set up in 1868 as a national association of all unions.

Dissatisfaction with the Liberal Party

The Liberals wanted the support of working class voters. They agreed with the model unions that working class candidates for Parliament should stand as Liberals in working class constituencies.

Members of the new unions, however, wanted something different. They wanted Parliament to help them in their struggles against employers, and to provide the working class with better houses, and schemes for unemployment and sickness benefit. The Liberal Party would not do any of this and also refused to increase the number of working class candidates at elections. The new unions asked the **Trades Union Congress** (TUC) to set up an organisation to send independent working class representatives to Parliament.

For many years the unions for skilled workers opposed this. Then, in the 1890s, employers started to attack their privileges and tried to reduce their wages. Also, judges in the law courts ruled that certain forms of strike action were illegal. In 1899 the union leaders changed their minds. They realised they too needed Parliament's help. They agreed to work with the socialists and the ILP to increase the number of Labour members in Parliament.

The Labour Representation Committee

In 1900 they set up the Labour Representation Committee (LRC) to organise Labour candidates for the next election. Fifteen candidates were put forward; only two were elected.

The LRC needed money from the trades unions to do its work, but by 1901 only a third of the unions had joined. Then a court ruling changed everything. In the **Taff Vale case** the court said that a union had to pay for any losses caused to a company by a strike.

This went against the right to strike that every union believed it had by law. Only Parliament could put this right. Every union now had an interest in supporting the LRC. By 1904 two thirds of them had joined. In the election of 1906 the LRC won twenty-nine seats. Working class candidates standing as Liberals won a further twenty-three. The two groups joined together in Parliament and called themselves the Labour Party.

i Taff Vale case   *The case was between the Taff Vale Railway Company and the Amalgamated Society of Railway Servants. The court fined the union £23,000.*

activity

1 Look at the information in the text on pages 98–100. Imagine you are a member of the LRC in 1902. Write a letter to the leader of a Union that has not yet joined explaining why it is important for the Union to join the LRC as soon as possible.

assignments

1 Use the sources and information on pages 82–84.
a Explain what you think (i) working class people (ii) middle class people (iii) Earl Grey wanted the Reform Act of 1832 to do for them.
b In each case say whether you think they got what they wanted. Give your reasons.

2 Use the sources and information on pages 80–86. Explain why you think the 1832 Reform Act is remembered as the 'Great' Reform Act.

3 Choose either the Chartists (pages 87–92) or the Fenians (pages 93–96) or the supporters of the formation of a Labour Party (pages 96–100). Write an article for a magazine about the group you have chosen explaining:
a The things they wanted to achieve,
b Whether you think they managed to achieve them. Give your reasons for your opinion.

4 Use the sources and information on pages 87–92.
a How do the different circumstances in which people lived and worked help to explain why some Chartists supported the use of physical force and others opposed it?
b What other factors might also help to explain this?

8 The Woman's Place

In Parts 2 and 4 you found out that the great changes brought about by the Industrial Revolution destroyed some traditional jobs and created many new ones. These changes affected the work done by women as well as by men. They also caused people to argue about whether or not women should work and, if so, what jobs they should do. In Part 8 you will look into some of these arguments and explore some of the attitudes to women that they reveal.

The 'perfect lady'

SOURCE 1

'Fact and Fiction; or Ye Bonny Fishwives of Scarborough and their Imitators', a cartoon for *Punch* drawn by George du Maurier in 1871.

During the nineteenth century, women lived in two different worlds (source 1). In one world were upper-class and middle-class women who were expected to live a life of leisure and to do no paid work. In the other world were working-class women who had to work whether they wanted to or not.

In the past, middle-class women had helped their husbands to run houses, estates and businesses. Some ran businesses on their own or took over when their husbands died.

activity

1 Look at source 1. Which group of women do you think the cartoonist prefers? Give your reasons.

activity

2 Look at source 4.
a Does it show that domestic plaiters and hat-makers were threatened by mass-production at the time it was painted?
b What can you learn from it about the plaiting and hat-making trade in 1891?

In the nineteenth century servants took over most of the chores and the organisation of the household, and clerks and assistants did the same in businesses.

The idea grew up of 'the perfect lady', elegant, well-dressed, and dependent on her father or husband because she should not work. The wives and daughters of middle-class men had to be seen to have plenty of leisure time. They used it to play music, to draw and paint and to do embroidery. Their place was at home.

Men described women as too 'delicate' to work. They praised their special 'feminine' qualities and often described them as 'angels'. According to William Gladstone:

SOURCE 2

If there be a subject . . . that is sacred [holy] . . . it is the character and position of women.

W. E. Gladstone, Speech in the House of Commons, 1884

In the 1850s some women began to challenge these ideas. Barbara Leigh Smith argued that through work women would find their rightful place in society:

SOURCE 3

A listless, idle, empty brained, empty hearted, ugly woman has no right to bear children. To think a woman is more feminine because she is frivolous, ignorant, weak, and sickly, is absurd.

Barbara Leigh Smith, *Women and Work*, 1857

SOURCE 4

A Bedfordshire straw hat workshop, painted in 1891. The grandmother is plaiting straw and the mother and daughter are making the plaits up into bonnets and hats. In the 1890s mass production in factories was putting many domestic plaiters and hat-makers out of business.

Working women

Working-class women had always had to work, either to earn their own living or to contribute to the upkeep of their families. Before the Industrial Revolution they mostly worked at home. By the 1850s the range of jobs they did was wider and many worked outside their own homes. Even so, large numbers still worked at home in domestic industries such as handloom weaving, pillow lace-making, straw plaiting (source 4), and stocking-, glove- and button-making.

Many women who worked outside their homes were in the dressmaking trade, often working long hours for low wages in small workshops. Others worked in the textile industry, many in factories. The textile factory workers were the best-paid women workers, though they were always paid less than men.

SOURCE 5

Domestic servants at Petworth House.

activity

I Look at sources 5, 6 and 7.
a Make a list of the points on which sources 6 and 7 (i) agree (ii) disagree.
b How do you explain the disgreements between them?
c How could source 5 be used to support (i) source 6 (ii) source 7?
2 Look at source 8. What can you tell about the artist's attitude to the women?

The largest number of all worked as domestic servants (source 5). Writers held different opinions about this kind of work:

SOURCE 6

The situation of a domestic servant . . . is attended with considerable comfort. With abundant work it combines a wonderful degree of . . . discipline, health, physical comfort . . .

J. D. Milne, *The Industrial and Social Position of Women*, 1857

SOURCE 7

Domestic service is incessant hard work at all hours of the day and sometimes of the night also. It is at best but a kind of slavery . . .

Emma Paterson, *The Organisation of Women's Industry*, 1879

Women also worked on the land. Their jobs included potato-gathering, turnip-pulling, hoeing, weeding, and picking fruit and vegetables. In the East Midlands and East Anglia girls often worked in agricultural gangs (source 8). An official from the Children's Employment Commission asked Georgina Rowan, who was sixteen, what kind of work was hardest, but she did not know. 'We're used to it now, and don't mind it', she said.

SOURCE 8

'The Stonepickers', painted by Sir George Clausen in 1887. This winter work was often given to women in agricultural gangs.

Women doing 'men's work': Wigan pit brow girls

Although it was accepted that working-class women had to work, there was a lot of discussion about what kind of jobs they should do. In the 1860s the House of Commons set up a Select Committee to investigate the case of women who worked on the surface of mines and collieries. One group, the pit brow girls of Wigan (source 9), wore trousers at work. The arguments about this particular group were especially fierce and reveal a lot about people's attitudes to women and to the sort of work that was thought suitable for them.

Unsuitable work for women

In 1864 the writer John Plummer visited Wigan to watch the pit girls at work. What he saw upset him:

SOURCE 10

In various directions might be witnessed women with bared arms, one or two with short pipes in their mouths, performing labours totally unsuited to their sex.

John Plummer, *Once A Week*, 27 August 1864

Plummer was not alone in thinking like this. Eight years earlier an official had reported on the work of pit girls in South Wales. He wrote of the 'masculine nature of the employment' which, he said, was 'degrading to female character'. He said that the girls became covered in dirt and this was bound to 'undermine their modesty and self-respect', and that working alongside men exposed them to bad language and bad habits.

All this, he said, meant that a pit girl was not able to carry out her proper functions in the home:

SOURCE 11

What is she able to do towards the management of a house, and towards making her husband happy and comfortable?
1 She does not know how to keep a house clean and tidy.
2 She cannot cook.
3 She knows nothing of the management required to make her husband's earnings go as far as possible.
4 She is ignorant of the proper management of children.

H. S. Tremenheere, Report of the South Wales Mining District, 1856

SOURCE 9

Pit brow girls at Shevington colliery near Wigan, photographed standing by a coal truck in 1867. Known in Lancashire as 'pit brow lasses' or 'broo wenches', their job was to push the pit wagons, which had come up from the mine loaded with coal, over the top of the pit brow and tip the coal into shoots where they removed the dirt from it. They also loaded railway trucks with coal.

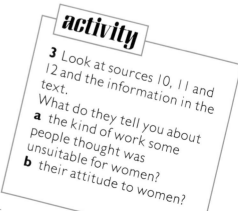

activity

3 Look at sources 10, 11 and 12 and the information in the text.
What do they tell you about
a the kind of work some people thought was unsuitable for women?
b their attitude to women?

Even some of the middle-class women who were looking for new ways forward for women agreed with some of these attitudes. Emily Faithfull included 'the loading of railway trucks' and 'dragging coal waggons' in a list of unsuitable jobs for women, saying:

SOURCE 12

We do not want to turn women into men, nor to see them doing men's work.

Emily Faithfull, 'The Unfit Employments in which Women are Engaged', *The Victoria Magazine*, 1863

Another writer argued that work on the pit brows was not 'unfeminine'. It provided the women with regular work and made them independent. As for bad language:

SOURCE 13

They hear on the pit mounds exactly the language they would hear at home, and much less of it, for work is not favourable to conversation.

The Edinburgh Review, April 1863

Trade union opposition

In 1842, Parliament passed a law banning the employment of women and children underground in coal mines. This followed the publication of the report of a commission of inquiry which showed that women and children were being forced to work in dreadful conditions. The report was illustrated and the public was horrified by the pictures as well as by the descriptions of what was going on (source 14).

SOURCE 14

A Woman working underground in a coal mine. An illustration from the First Report of the Children's Employment Commission (on mines), 1842.

Male miners had other reasons for opposing the employment of women and children in mines. Women and children were paid less than men. Employers could use this cheaper labour either to put men out of work or to force them to work for lower wages themselves. So the miners' trade unions, which men could join and women could not, campaigned hard against the employment of women:

SOURCE 15

Keep them at home . . . to look after their families . . . there is then some chance of a higher rate of wages being enforced.

Miners Association of Great Britain and Ireland, 1842

After 1842 women could still work on the surface of coal mines. The miners' unions were determined to get rid of them even from there. In 1865 the miners of Northumberland and Durham petitioned Parliament about several matters, including the employment of women as surface labourers. They claimed it was degrading for women to do this kind of work. It was this petition which led the House of Commons to set up a Select Committee to look into the matters raised by the miners.

Evidence to the Select Committee

The Select Committee interviewed people between 1865 and 1867. William Pickard, the Miners' Agent (union representative) of the Wigan District, strongly opposed women working on the pit brow. He was asked what exactly it was about the work that degraded women. He replied:

SOURCE 16

If they are employed from six o'clock in the morning to five or six at night, their absence from home leaves domestic duties entirely in a jumblement [in confusion]; and when the husband comes home it leads to much unpleasantness and much altercation [argument], and leads the men to go and spend their time elsewhere.

Report from the Select Committee on Mines, 1866

This surprised the MP who had asked the question. He said he could see how the the women's work might be inconvenient to their husbands, but that did not explain why it should be described as 'degrading' to the women.

Pickard could only repeat that pit brow work did not allow women to carry out their home duties 'as satisfactorily as they ought'. Then he suggested that the women could find alternative 'honourable employment' in factories (source 17) or in domestic service. This was a contradiction, since work of this kind would also have taken the women out of the home. If Pickard noticed it, he did not say so.

SOURCE 17

'The Dinner Hour: Wigan', painted by Eyre Crowe in 1874.

An MP asked Peter Dickinson, a miner from Aspull near Wigan, about the pit brow girls' working clothes: 'It is rather [like] a man's dress that they wear, is it not?' Dickinson agreed:

SOURCE 18

It is rather a man's dress; and I believe, in some cases, it drowns all sense of decency betwixt men and women ...

Report from the Select Committee on Mines, 1866

Questioned further, Dickinson agreed it was the most convenient form of dress for the type of work. Then the MP pointed out that 'the entire person is covered, and there is nothing indecent in the dress.' So why, he asked, did Dickinson speak of it as one of the main things that made the girls' work degrading? He answered:

SOURCE 19

It clothes the person, but it does not drown the feeling.

Report from the Select Committee on Mines, 1866

Final victory

In 1867 the Select Committee decided to take no action against the employment of pit brow girls. It felt there was very little difference between the work they did and that done by many other women working out of doors, for example on farms or in ironworks.

activity

1 Look at sources 5, 9 and 17 and the information in the text. Why do you think William Pickard thought of domestic service and factory work, but not pit brow work, as 'honourable employment'?
2 Look at sources 16, 18 and 19 and the information in the text on pages 106–108.
a How does the information about trades unions help to explain William Pickard's and Peter Dickinson's statements to the Select Committee?
b How do the questions they were asked suggest that members of the Select Committee were probably not convinced by their arguments?

It thought the work was 'obviously unfitted for women' but to ban it when there was no other work available would cause 'a great deal of grievous suffering'.

Nineteen years later the pit brow girls were attacked again. The newspaper reports of the time suggest that the unions' arguments were the same as before but that public opinion was beginning to change. The *Daily Telegraph* challenged the unions:

SOURCE 20

An attempt is being made by labour representatives in and out of the House of Commons to have a clause inserted into the Mines' Regulations Bill prohibiting female labour at the pit's brow, and it is urged [argued] that this is being done in the interests of the women themselves ... Are these ... real or pretended champions of women?

The *Daily Telegraph*, 23 March 1886

The *Birmingham Post* took up the question of the pit girls' trousers:

SOURCE 21

From the indignant terms in which the pit girls' costume is denounced by some of the labour representatives, one would suppose that it was something in the nature of a ballet dress ...

The *Birmingham Post*, quoted in the *Wigan Observer and District Advertiser*, 26 March 1886

It went on to say it was ridiculous to prevent pit girls:

SOURCE 22

From earning an honest living on account of the immodesty of their attire, whilst suffering [allowing] high bred ladies to go to a ball or a drawing room with the most delicate parts of their bodies fully exposed ...

The *Birmingham Post*, quoted in the *Wigan Observer and District Advertiser*, 26 March 1886

In 1887 a deputation of pit brow girls travelled to London to see the Home Secretary. He told them he would not interfere with their work other than to make it illegal for them to be employed to move railway wagons.

activity

3 How do sources 20, 21 and 22 suggest that public opinion about the pit brow girls was beginning to change?

The women's rights movement

activity

1 Look at sources 23 and 24 and the information in the text and at the sources and information on page 103. Write what you think Harriet Taylor Mill might have written about the idea of the 'perfect lady'

From about 1850 some educated middle-class women began to argue against the idea that a woman should be a 'perfect lady' (see page 103). They thought all women should be allowed to work, and to have the same legal and voting rights as men.

In 1847 Anne Knight joined with seven Chartist women in Sheffield to form the first 'Female Political Association' to campaign for women to have the vote. In the 1850s Harriet Taylor Mill wrote essays arguing for women's rights. She attacked the view of women as people too special to be allowed to take part in the hurly-burly of the real world:

SOURCE 23

What is wanted for women is equal rights, equal admission to all social privileges . . .

Harriet Taylor Mill, *Enfranchisement of Women*, 1851

She compared men to slave-owners and women to slaves:

SOURCE 24

The real question is whether it is right and expedient [useful] that one-half of the human race should pass through life in an enforced subordination [controlled by] to the other half.

Harriet Taylor Mill, *Enfranchisement of Women*, 1851

The law said that when a woman married she lost all rights to her own money and property. As a result of women's campaigns, Parliament passed new laws allowing married women to do what they liked with the money they earned (1878), and to keep control of their own property (1882).

Women also campaigned for the right to study for and take exams at universities. They founded women's colleges at the universities of Oxford, Cambridge and London. In 1866 Elizabeth Garrett Anderson became the first British woman to qualify as a doctor.

In 1865 the first organisation to campaign for women to have the right to vote was formed. The next year 80 MPs voted in favour of women having the vote, but the majority of the Liberal Party, which women hoped would support them, continued to oppose the idea.

In 1897 all the various women's rights societies formed into the National Union of Women's Suffrage Societies. This was led by Millicent Fawcett, Elizabeth Garrett Anderson's sister. From this time onwards working-class women joined the campaign, too. In 1900, over 29,000 female Lancashire factory workers signed a petition demanding the vote because, they said, not having it lowered their position in relation to men, both at home and at work.

By 1900 women had won the right to be town councillors and to vote in local elections provided they had the right amount of property. The campaign to win the right to vote in national elections went on for more than 20 years.

assignments

I Use the sources and information in Part 8.
a Explain how (i) cartoons (ii) government reports (iii) newspapers can be used to investigate attitudes to women and work in the nineteenth century.
b What do you think are (i) the advantages (ii) the disadvantages of

- drawings and paintings
- photographs
- written sources

as evidence for that investigation?

2 Use the sources and information on pages 105–109.
a How reliable do you think William Pickard's statements to the Select Committee were as evidence about the pit brow girls' work? Explain your reasons as fully as possible.
b What uses do his statements have for an historian as evidence in an investigation into the work of the pit brow girls?

3 Suppose a reporter is able to go back in time from the present to the mid-nineteenth century to make a radio or television documentary about different people's attitudes to women and work. The reporter decides to interview:
a The husband of a 'perfect lady' (page 103)
b Barbara Leigh Smith (page 103)
c One of the pit brow girls in source 10
d Emily Faithfull (page 106)
e William Pickard (page 107)
Write what you think each of them would tell the reporter.

9
Religion and Reform

Religion was still important to many people in the nineteenth century, though many working class people did not go to church because they felt the Church of England was out of touch with their lives. New types of Churches started up and there was a revival in religious belief which also helped to bring about social reform.

The Churches

Churchgoing

On Sunday, 30 March 1851, for the first and only time, a census (count) was taken of all the people in England and Wales who went to church. These were the figures:

SOURCE 1

Church of England	*3.5 million*
Methodist	*2 million*
Other Nonconformists	*1.5 million*
Roman Catholics	*.25 million*
Non-attenders	*6.5 million*

The census showed that the numbers of people going to Church of England and Nonconformist services that day were about equal. It also showed that just under half of those who might have gone to

---

activity

1 Look at source 1 and the information in the text. As evidence of the churchgoing habits of the people of the time, what do you think are
a the strengths
b the weaknesses of the census of 30 March 1851?
Give your reasons.

activity

2 How do sources 3 and 4 suggest that the Church of England was mainly for the middle classes?

3 What might an Evangelical have felt on reading source 3?

church did not. In some big towns this figure was about 75 per cent. According to the official report on the census:

SOURCE 2

The masses of our working population are never, or but seldom [only occasionally], seen in our religious congregations.

H. Mann, *Religious Worship in England and Wales*, 1854

The Church of England

The Church of England was supposed to be the country's main Church. Why did it appeal to only half of the Protestants in England and Wales? The main reason was that during the eighteenth and early nineteenth centuries it had gradually lost touch with working-class people. It was still strong in much of the countryside, but in the large new towns it was only one Church among many.

By 1851 the Church of England mainly looked after the needs of middle-class people. What was happening in churches in Ipswich was typical of others throughout the country:

SOURCE 3

Some of the pews for the rich were padded, lined, cushioned, and supplied with every comfort . . . The poor, on the other hand, were seated on stools in the aisles; many of the seats were without backs, to prevent the occupants from falling asleep during the sermon . . .

John Glyde, *The Moral, Social and Religious Condition of Ipswich*, 1850

For many of the middle class, going to church was a social event (source 4). They thought of themselves as 'respectable' and showed this in the clothes they wore. Many working people felt shut out because the middle classes did not consider them to be respectable, nor did they wish to be seen at church in their poorer clothes.

Despite all this, some Church of England vicars and bishops tried very hard to look after working people. In the 1830s parishes were created in the new industrial towns. Many priests campaigned for reforms that would improve the living and working conditions of their parishioners.

There was also a strong group of people in the Church of England called the 'Evangelicals'. They believed the Church was for everyone and that what people looked like or how they dressed did not matter. The Evangelicals were middle-class people who wanted to take the message of Christianity to working-class people and to the poor. They wanted to help people who were less well-off than themselves.

SOURCE 4

A Church of England vicar greets his congregation at Christmas.

Nonconformists

Nonconformists worshipped in chapels rather than churches (source 5). They were strongest in the new industrial areas of the north of England, in Wales, and in Devon and Cornwall. The various different groups all shared a belief in the importance of reading and studying the Bible, and of listening to sermons. They were strong supporters of Sunday schools. Strict Nonconformists disapproved of dancing, card playing and the drinking of alchohol, especially on Sundays.

SOURCE 5

Capel Eglwysbach, Berw Road, Pontypridd. Congregations had to pay for the building of their own chapels, so many were quite simple in structure. This one in South Wales is very imposing. It was built in the later nineteenth century when many better-off people such as the colliery owners and managers were Nonconformists. The chapel was a community centre as well as a place of worship. Many people who were not chapel-goers would have used it for social activities such as choir practices and drama groups.

activity

I What does source 5 tell you about the strength of Nonconformist groups in Wales?

Methodists

By 1851 the Methodists were by far the largest Nonconformist group. They began in the eighteenth century as a group within the Church of England. In 1829 John Wesley, a Church of England priest, founded the Methodist Society. He believed that the Church was for all classes of people and he used dramatic sermons and hymn singing to inspire ordinary working people in the towns and the countryside to live Christian lives.

activity

2 What can you learn from sources 6 and 7, and the information in the text, about
a the ways in which Methodism was attractive to working-class people?
b the weaknesses of the Church of England?
3 Look at source 7. Explain why you think the colliery owners supported the Methodists.

Some members of the Church of England did not like Wesley's methods. He was often forbidden to preach in churches and so he started to hold open-air services in which he preached to masses of people. After Wesley's death in 1791 his followers broke from the Church of England altogether and set up a separate Methodist Church.

In the early nineteenth century the Methodists took their message to poor and working-class people in industrial areas where the Church of England was weak. Methodism gave many people a new sense of purpose and a feeling of community spirit. In 1840 a Methodist minister wrote of its influence in East Yorkshire:

SOURCE 6

Thousands who had sunk to a level of dull monotony, unbroken . . . except by fairs, races . . . found in our . . . soul stirring preaching services, fervent prayer meetings, lively class-meetings and hearty singing . . . a life, a freedom, and a joy to which they had been strangers . . . Indeed, Methodist chapels have long been the centres around which the religious life of these villages has revolved. They feel at home there as they do not at the Parish Church.

Quoted in V. T. J. Arkell, *Britain Transformed*, 1973

Another writer reported that colliery owners in the districts of Northumberland and Durham encouraged Methodists because:

SOURCE 7

The colliery people were collected in places mostly lying apart from the established parish churches, which then had no curates or scripture readers going forth to reach such people. The owners wisely facilitated [helped] the operations of the Wesleyans in opening Sunday Schools and chapels. Many of the colliers became local preachers . . .

R. Lowery, *The Weekly Record*, 1856

Roman Catholics

During much of the eighteenth century, Catholics continued to be hated by many people, as they had been in the seventeenth century. They were forbidden to hold government office or to vote.

Towards the end of the century things slowly began to change. Catholics in Ireland won the right to vote in 1793; Catholics in Britain won it in 1807. In 1829, after fierce debates, Parliament passed a law which allowed Catholics to hold office in both local and national government and to become MPs.

The number of Catholics in England increased in the nineteenth century, partly because of the immigration of many Irish people. They settled mainly in Liverpool, in other northern industrial towns, and in London.

The abolition of the slave trade

Between 1750 and 1900 many reformers campaigned to change the law in order to improve the conditions in which various people lived and worked. Others set up schemes of their own. Some of these reformers, though not all, had religious motives for their work. In this and the following case study, try to work out what part religious belief played in helping to bring about reforms.

In 1807 Parliament passed the Abolition Act which outlawed the trade in slaves from 1 January 1808. Twenty-five years later it passed the Emancipation Act which freed all slaves in the British Empire and outlawed slavery. This case study is about the campaign which led to the passing of the first of these two Acts.

The slave trade

The British had been involved in the slave trade between Africa and the Caribbean and North America since the early seventeenth century. By the mid-eighteenth century it played an important part in Britain's overall pattern of trade (see pages 54–58). It is estimated that in 1768, for example, British vessels shipped more than 50,000 slaves across the Atlantic. The conditions in these ships were very bad and hundreds of slaves died during the crossing (source 8a).

Opposition to slavery

During the eighteenth century a few people in Britain began to speak out against the keeping of slaves. Not all the people who opposed slavery were religious, but the leadership of the campaign against slavery and the slave trade did come from a religious group, the Quakers.

The Quakers were members of the Society of Friends, founded by George Fox in the seventeeth century. They believed the spirit of God was in each person, so they did not believe in priests or churches. They held religious meetings in ordinary buildings. They dressed simply and avoided games and amusements. They refused to use violence.

George Fox told Quakers who emigrated to Pennsylvania and the Caribbean to welcome their slaves to religious meetings, to treat them kindly and to release them after a certain time. This made

activity

1a Use the information on pages 113 (the Evangelicals) and 116 (the Quakers) to explain why you think (i) the Evangelicals, (ii) the Quakers opposed slavery.
b Look at sources 8 and 9. What do you think (i) supporters, (ii) opponents of slavery would have said about each one?

SOURCE 8a

Plan of a slave ship, showing how as many slaves as possible were crowded in. The bottom diagram shows the lower deck. The top one shows a platform fixed around the ship's walls between the lower and upper decks.

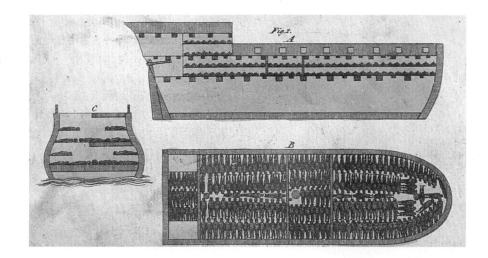

SOURCE 8b

Slave huts on a sugar plantation in St John's, Antigua. The huts were made of wattle, daub and thatch. Slaves usually worked a sixteen and a half hour day in either the fields or the sugar factory.

them unpopular with other slave owners. In Britain, the Quakers' London meeting decided to oppose the slave trade in 1727. In 1761 they expelled any Quakers found still to be involved in the trade.

The Committee for the Abolition of the Slave Trade

The next move came from a member of the Church of England called Glanville Sharp. Sharp was an Evangelical (see page 113). He knew there were thousands of slaves in Britain, mostly brought over from the Caribbean. They were even bought and sold:

SOURCE 9

For sale at the Bull and Gate Inn, Holborn, a chestnut gelding, a tin whistle, and a well made, good tempered Black Boy.

Advertisement in the *Gazette*, April 1769

A china medallion produced in support of the anti-slavery campaign by Josiah Wedgwood's pottery works.

> **ⓘ Josiah Wedgwood**
> *Josiah Wedgwood (1730–95) opened his first pottery in 1759. Between 1768 and 1769 he built a factory and village for his workers named Etruria, now in Stoke-on-Trent. He built schools and wanted his workers to have good living conditions. As well as developing different types of pottery he helped to improve roads and canals.*

activity

1 How do you think source 11 helped the anti-slave trade campaign?
2 The information in the text on this page explains how changing circumstances between 1783 and 1807 helped Wilberforce in his campaign. Make a list of the changes and say how each one helped Wilberforce.

Sharp believed slavery was illegal in Britain. In 1772 he managed to get a judge to give a ruling. The judge agreed that English law did not recognise slavery. The Quakers then formed an anti-slavery society to oppose slavery in the colonies.

After many discussions the members of the society decided that the best way to end slavery would be to end the slave trade itself, cutting off the supply of slaves to the plantations. In 1787 the society was renamed the 'Committeee for the Abolition of the Slave Trade'. Most of its members were Quakers or Evangelicals. One of the Evangelicals, William Wilberforce, agreed to lead the campaign.

Supporters and opponents

A member of the Committee called Thomas Clarkson was sent to Liverpool and Bristol to find out all he could about the slave ships. He spoke to twenty thousand sailors. The stories he heard provided evidence of the horrors of the trade. Many people started to support the campaign. **Josiah Wedgwood**, the owner of a pottery company, had china medallions made which were decorated with the words 'Am I not a man and a brother (source 10).

The owners of slave ships and plantations opposed the campaign. They were supported by many MPs. Wilberforce's proposal to abolish the slave trade was defeated twice and then held up because war broke out with France in 1793. The Prime Minister, William Pitt, claimed he did not want Parliament arguing about other issues while Britain was fighting a war.

Success

Despite the war, Wilberforce proposed abolition many times, but he was always defeated. Gradually, however, circumstances changed. During the war against France the British Empire increased (see Part 5, page 55). The trade with the Caribbean started to become less important than the trade with other new areas (see page 58).

Many MPs now represented the interests of merchants trading with India and the East. The goods they traded were not produced with slave labour. They were prepared to vote against the slave trade.

Even some planters in the West Indies began to support abolition. Britain had conquered new Caribbean islands in the war. If these were to start to produce sugar, too, there would be too much on the market and profits, already beginning to fall, would collapse altogether. Without the help of more slaves from Africa the new conquests could not become sugar producers.

Encouraged by a new Prime Minister, Charles James Fox, Parliament finally passed the Abolition Act in 1807. The slave trade was to be illegal from 1 January 1808.

SOURCE 11

Lord Shaftesbury. His title was Lord Ashley until 1851 when he became the Earl of Shaftesbury. As well as supporting factory reform he campaigned for better conditions for colliery workers and chimney sweeps, and for better housing for the poor. He was chairman of the Royal Commission to investigate working conditions in mines and introduced into the House of Commons the bill that became the 1842 Mines Act.

Social conditions

In Parts 2 and 4 you found out about the dreadful conditions in which people had to live and work in the cities and factories that grew up as a result of the Industrial Revolution. Throughout the nineteenth century some people were very concerned about these problems and tried to find solutions to them. This case study is about some of the ideas and reforms that they produced.

Factory reform

Both adults and children had to work extremely long hours in the factories (see Part 4, pages 45–47). In 1831 the Ten Hours Movement was formed to campaign for a ten hour working day for everyone. The leader of the movement was Richard Oastler, who was a member of Church of England and an Evangelical. He compared the treatment of children in factories to the treatment of slaves in the colonies:

SOURCE 12

Thousands of little children . . . are daily compelled to labour, from six o'clock in the morning to seven in the evening with only . . . thirty minutes alowed for eating and recreation.

Richard Oastler, Letter to the 'Leeds Mercury', 16 October 1830

To get the law changed Oastler needed help in the House of Commons. First Michael Sadler and then Lord Shaftesbury (source 11) agreed to lead the Ten Hour Movement in Parliament. Both were Evangelicals. Shaftesbury once wrote in his diary that he wanted to contribute to:

SOURCE 13

The advancement of religion and the increase of human happiness.

Lord Shaftesbury, Diary, 17 December 1827

In 1833 the government set up a Royal Commission to examine the matter. Many people believed it was wrong for the government to interfere in the relationship between employers and workers. They thought that workers should be allowed to work long hours if they wished. The employers argued that if people did not work so for long, factories would not be able to produce so much. They said this would damage profits and, therefore, in the end they would have to pay the workers lower wages.

activity

3 Use source 13 and the information about the Evangelicals on page 113. Why might Shaftesbury have agreed to support the Ten Hours Movement?

4 Use the sources and information in the text.

a What were the arguments (i) for, and (ii) against the Government passing laws to reduce working hours in textile factories?

b Which side do you think had the better case? Give your reasons.

activity

1 What does source 14 tell you about why employers began to change their minds about the length of working hours?

2 The 1844 Act limited the hours that women (as well as children) could work. Why was this an important change?

3 Look at the information about the Acts of 1833, 1847 and 1850. Do you think the 1850 Act was a victory for the Ten Hours Movement or for the employers? Discuss your ideas in a group.

The Royal Commission agreed that it was wrong for the government to interfere with the working hours of adults. But it said the government ought to interfere in the case of children. In 1833 a Factory Act was passed (source 14). This Act did not make a big difference. The employers found it easy to get round and there were too few inspectors. But it did show that the government was prepared to make laws about working conditions.

The leaders of the Ten Hours Movement were disappointed because the 1833 Act left out women and men. Eleven years later there was another Factory Act (source 14), but Shaftesbury was again defeated in trying to get a Ten Hours rule included.

SOURCE 14

1833
• no child under 9 years could work at all • children aged 9 to 13 could work up to 9 hours a day • children aged 14 to 18 could work up to 12 hours per day • children under 13 had to attend school for 2 hours per day • 4 inspectors were to be appointed to check on all this
1844
• children aged 8 and above were now allowed to work • children aged 8 to 13 could only work for 6½ hours a day • children aged 14 to 18, and women, could only work a 12 hour day • mill owners were to put safety fences round dangerous machinery

The factory acts of 1833 and 1844.

Gradually many factory owners began to change their minds. They realised that workers could produce as much work in shorter hours. One of them pointed out that the last two hours were often wasted anyway:

SOURCE 15

There is more bad work made in the last one or two hours of the day than the whole of the first nine or ten hours,

Robert Gardner, Letter, 22 April 1845

In 1847 a further Act reduced the hours of women and children to ten, but the employers then worked them in a relay system and increased mens' hours to make up the difference. Finally Shaftesbury proposed a compromise. The 1850 Act established a ten and a half hour day for all, children, women and men. Like all previous Acts it applied only to textile factories, but it created an important principle.

Model employers

Some employers were reformers themselves. They are known as 'model employers' because they set up model ways of doing things.

Robert Owen and the New Lanark Mills

Robert Owen became general manager and part-owner of David Dale's New Lanark Mills in Scotland in 1799. He believed people worked best when their living and working conditions were good. He therefore limited the working day in the mill to ten and a half hours. No child under ten was allowed to work at all. Workers were paid when they were sick. He built good houses for the workers and set up schools for their children.

Sir Titus Salt and Saltaire

Sir Titus Salt was a Bradford manufacturer. In 1850 he rebuilt his woollen mills three miles outside Bradford in Airedale beside the River Aire. He built houses for his employees nearby and called the whole development 'Saltaire' (source 16). The facilities he provided included a Nonconformist church, a hospital, schools, houses for elderly and sick people, a club, a library, and a public park. He would not allow a public house. By 1880 about 4,400 people lived in Saltaire.

SOURCE 16

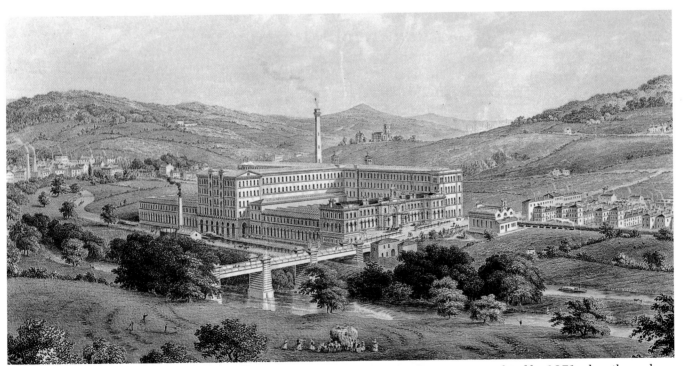

Saltaire in about 1860. The new factory opened in 1853. The town surrounding it was completed by 1871 when the park was opened.

George Cadbury and Bournville

George Cadbury came from a strict Quaker background. He would not even allow an easy chair into his house until he was over seventy. He believed that it was a sin to build up a large amount of personal wealth. He thought money should be used for the benefit of other people. He also believed that it was useless to tell people who lived in slums to lead good lives. First, he said, you must improve their living conditions.

With his brother Richard he took over a small chocolate factory in Birmingham which his father, John Cadbury, had set up as a branch of his tea and coffee business. They made it very successful. In the 1870s they decided to move the factory away from the centre of Birmingham because they needed to make it larger.

The new site had plenty of space, fresh air and good water, but it was hard for workers to reach. So, as well as a new factory, he built Bournville Village where they could live. The houses were carefully planned and each one had a garden. Cadbury believed gardens were important because they helped people to relax, provided vegetables to eat, and kept men out of pubs and with their families. There were also cricket and football fields.

The company also provided its workers with a pension scheme to give them money in their old age, and medical and dental care. George Cadbury wanted his company to show how industry should be run for the good of everyone. He also managed to show that an employer who took care of his workers could still make good profits.

activity

1 Use the information in the text on pages 119–120 and on page 122.
a What arguments against George Cadbury's ideas about running a business do you think other employers might have used?
b Write the letter which you think George Cadbury might have sent to one of them to persuade him to change his mind.

Public health reform

In Part 2 (pages 17–18) you found out about the dirty and unhealthy conditions in which people lived in the new industrial towns. These led to outbreaks of diseases such as typhus and cholera. Cholera was a new disease in Britain and greatly feared. The first epidemic in 1831–2 killed 31,000 people; the second in 1848–9 killed 62,000.

Cholera was a disease of the intestine caused by polluted water, but people did not know this at the time. Instead doctors believed that the illness was caused by breathing in bad air that had been poisoned by filth (source 17).

In 1842 Edwin Chadwick, one of the Poor Law Commissioners (see page 88), produced a 'Report on the Sanitary Conditions of the Labouring Population'. Chadwick believed the 'bad air theory' and said that the answer was to get rid of the filth. He recommended that streets should be cleaned and their drains improved. Sewers should be built, and pure running water supplied.

Chadwick agreed with the ideas of a thinker called Jeremy Bentham. He had been Bentham's secretary until his death in 1832.

SOURCE 17

'A Court for King Cholera', a cartoon in *Punch*, 1852. During the third epidemic, 1853–4, Dr John Snow studied cases of cholera in Golden Square, London. He showed that the victims lived near water pumps polluted by sewage rather than near ones that were not. This showed that polluted water caused the disease. Many doctors did not accept this theory until after another epidemic killed 6,000 Londoners in 1866. The cholera virus itself was discovered in 1884.

activity

2 Look at the information in the text. Edwin Chadwick and Lord Shaftesbury were both reformers.
a What motives did they have in common?
b How were their motives different?
3 Look at source 17 and the information in the text.
a Make a list of the reasons why people (i) supported (ii) opposed public health reform.
b Write (i) a letter to a local newspaper from an opponent of the 1848 Public Health Act (ii) a reply from a supporter.

Bentham believed that it was wrong to allow people to run their lives as they wished without the Government interfering. He thought the Government ought to make laws in order to improve the lives of as many people as possible. He said that the purpose of a law was to bring the greatest happiness to the greatest number of people.

Most people at this time disagreed with this. They believed that the Government should not tell men and women how to run their lives. They genuinely believed people were happiest when left alone to run their lives as they wished. It also suited some people to use this argument when their own interests were threatened. The mill owners used it against the Factory Acts. Private water companies and sewage disposal contractors, who were paid to take sewage away in carts, used it to attack Chadwick's proposals.

In 1848 Parliament passed a Public Health Act. Towns were to build sewers, keep streets cleaned, install lighting and see that houses were built with drains and connected to water supplies. Many did not do this because most people had very little interest in public health except when there was a cholera outbreak, and rate payers complained about the costs.

Two more Acts, in 1866 and 1875, compelled town councils to provide water, sewage and drainage services and to appoint Medical Oficers of Health, but in many areas facilities for the poorest people did not improve until well into the twentieth century.

assignments

1 Use the sources and information on pages 113–115. Why do you think so many working class people chose to become Methodists rather than to join the Church of England?

2 Choose either the abolition of the slave trade (pages 116–118) or social reform (pages 119–123). Use the appropriate sources and information.
a Make a list of (i) factors to do with religion (ii) other factors which helped to bring about change in the case study you have chosen. Write a few lines about each factor.
b How important do you think religious belief was in bringing about these changes? Explain your reasons as fully as possible.

3 Use the sources and information on pages 119–120 and 121–123.
a Which groups of people (i) supported (ii) opposed factory reform?
b What links can you find between people's circumstances and their attitude to factory reform?
c Robert Owen's attitude was different from most mill owners of his time. What reasons did he have for this?

4 Use the sources and information on pages 122–123.
a Make a list (i) of the ways in which Edwin Chadwick helped to bring about improvements in public health (ii) of other factors which helped.
b How important do you think the role of Edwin Chadwick was in bringing about public health reform in the nineteenth century? Explain your reasons as fully as possible.
c Do you think Chadwick was successful in his campaign to reform public health? Explain your reasons.

The death of Queen Victoria

On Tuesday, **1 January 1901**, Queen Victoria's subjects celebrated New Year's Day and the start of a new century. Three weeks later, on 22 January, the Queen died. She was 82 years old. She had been Queen since 1837, when she was 18, a reign of 64 years.

Most people could remember no other monarch. Victoria stood for Britain and the Empire, and for the achievements of the British people during her reign. In 1887 and 1897 her Golden and Diamond Jubilees had been celebrated with enthusiasm in Britain and throughout the Empire (source 1). To many, the day of her death seemed like the end of an era.

i **1 January 1901** Some people thought the start of the twentieth century should have been celebrated on 1 January 1900. But the first year of the era AD was 1 AD not 0 AD, so the first 100 years of the era were completed at the end of 100 AD. Thus 101 AD was the first year of the second century, and 1901 AD was the first year of the twentieth century.

Taking stock

The turn of the century had already caused people to think about the changes that had taken place over the last hundred years. The death of the Queen made them even more inclined to look back and take stock. Many were struck by the changes that had taken place as a result of the numerous inventions of the time; but they disagreed about whether or not these changes had led to progress.

A. R. Wallace, a scientist, called the nineteenth century as a whole 'the wonderful century'. He agreed with others who said that Britain had been transformed into a new country. The writer, H. G. Wells, said that the people of Victoria's time were:

SOURCE 2

Overtaken by power, by possessions and great new freedoms, and unable to make any civilised use of them at all.

Quoted by Asa Briggs in *The Cambridge Historical Encyclopedia of Great Britain and Ireland*, 1985

There had been other changes, too. When Victoria became Queen in 1837, her typical subject lived in the countryside; by the time she died, her typical subject was a town dweller. Less than a quarter of the population lived in rural areas in 1901.

SOURCE 1

Celebrations in Norfolk for Victoria's Diamond Jubilee, 1897.

activity

1 Look at source 2 and the information in the text.
a Use your knowledge of the nineteenth century to make a list of arguments that support the views of
(i) A. R. Wallace,
(ii) H. G. Wells.
b (i) Discuss these arguments in a group.
(ii) Decide which view you most support. Give your reasons.

Young men, in particular, were leaving the countryside. According to one Wiltshire farmer:

SOURCE 3

Young men . . . are now seldom to be seen upon the land, while hedgers, ditchers and thatchers are all over fifty years of age.

Quoted in P. Horn, *Labouring Life in the Victorian Countryside*, 1976

In 1837 the Great Reform Act had been law for five years and the Chartist movement was just beginning; by 1901 two more Reform Acts had been passed but Britain was still not a full democracy. Many men and all women had yet to win the right to vote.

In 1837 Britian was the leading, almost the only, industrial nation of the world. The Great Exhibition of 1851 celebrated the supremacy of the British and demonstrated their self-confidence. In 1901 the British merchants and the owners of factories were less confident. Britain was one industrial country among many. Its rivals were catching up.

In 1837 the Empire was strong and about to grow larger; in 1901 it was at its largest and few people would have dreamt of it ever becoming smaller. Yet in India demands for self-rule were growing. Within less than fifty years India was to become independent.

The beginning of an era?

Looking back from the 1990s, what is striking about the 1890s is not so much that they saw the ending of an era but that, in some ways, they saw the beginning of one. This is especially the case in the field of transport and communications. Here the 1890s saw the appearance of inventions which went on to become an essential part of people's lives in the twentieth century.

For men and women of all classes, in the countryside as well as the town, one of the most important inventions was the bicycle (source 4). Although they had been invented earlier, bicycles became fairly cheap to buy in the 1890s. They gave their owners the freedom to move about and see new places.

They gave many young working-class men and women in the countryside their first chance to travel some distance away from their own village whenever they wished. People living in towns used them to visit the countryside.

SOURCE 4

Chelmsford Ladies Cycling Club, 1890. A bicycle driven by pedals, cranks and rods was in use in Scotland in about 1839. The first chain driven model with an equal-size rear wheel was made in England in 1885. The pneumatic tyre was invented in Scotland in 1888.

Bicycles took middle-class girls out of the drawing room and into the open air. *The Musical Times* blamed them for a drop in the popularity of piano playing:

SOURCE 5

There are literally thousands of young ladies whose leisure hours, formerly passed in large part on the music stool, are now spent in the saddle of the 'iron bird' as a lady journalist has poetically described the bicycle.

The Musical Times, 1896

After the bicycle came the petrol-driven motor car (source 6). This was first developed in France and Germany. The first British engine was produced in 1888 and the first four-wheeler car in 1895. In the same year Herbert Austin designed a car that was built in Birmingham by the Wolsely Sheep Shearing Company. Unlike bicycles, cars were for the very wealthy, and were to remain so until well into the twentieth century.

Electric trams started to run in many cities in the 1890s. Petrol-driven motor taxis were introduced in London in 1905, and public motor buses appeared two years later.

SOURCE 6

A motor car in a London Street in 1900.

activity

2 What can you work out from sources 4 and 5, and the information in the text, about the effect of the bicycle on the lives of women?

SOURCE 7

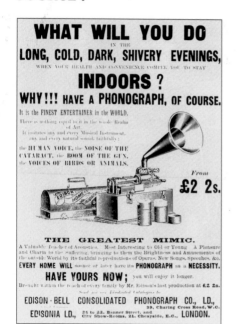

An advertisement for an Edison Home Phonograph from the illustrated London News, 1899.

In the 1870s a machine called a 'phonograph' was invented by Thomas Edison. By the 1890s it was being mass-produced (source 7). It was also given a new name, the gramophone. The word 'record' first came into use in 1896.

Another invention of the 1870s was also developed in the 1890s. This was Alexander Graham Bell's telephone. The Post Office already ran a national telegraph system which allowed people to have messages sent by **Morse code** along telegraph wires connecting Post Offices in towns and villages. In 1890 it allowed the private National Telephone Company to be formed to set up a telephone network (source 8).

To begin with, telephones, like cars, were for the well-off. Queen Victoria, who had sent messages by telegraph at the Great Exhibition in 1851, was one of the first to have this latest invention installed forty years later.

SOURCE 8

The National Telephone Company's exchange, installed in 1900. The Post Office took over the running of the long-distance network in 1892 and of the whole system in 1904.

i **Morse code** A system of sending messages named after its American inventor, Samuel Morse (1791–1872). 'Dots' and 'dashes' can be transmitted by flashlight or by sending electrical impulses along a wire. A dash is three times as long as a dot. Combinations of dots and dashes stand for letters of the alphabet and for numbers.

activity

1 What information does source 8 give you about women and work in 1900?
2a How do the sources and information on pages 126–128 suggest that the 1890s saw the beginning of an era?
b Do you think (i) the turn of the century, (ii) the death of Queen Victoria in 1901 were important events? Give your reasons.